CHILD CARE NOW

PUBLISHED BY
BRITISH AGENCIES FOR
ADOPTION & FOSTERING
11 SOUTHWARK STREET
LONDON SE1 1RQ
© BAAF 1989
ISBN 0 903534 85 1
DESIGNED BY ANDREW HAIG
TYPESET BY ETHNOGRAPHICA
PRINTED BY ASHDOWN PRESS

RESEARCH SERIES: 6

Child care now

a survey of placement patterns

Jane Rowe, Marion Hundleby
and Louise Garnett

BRITISH AGENCIES FOR
ADOPTION & FOSTERING

Acknowledgements

Few research projects can have been so indebted to so many social workers and administrative staff as ours has been. Without the continued interest and cooperation of hundreds of individuals in our six project authorities, this study could not have been successfully completed. We are deeply grateful to all of them. Thanks are also due to the directors and managers in the six authorities for agreeing to take part and for making the necessary arrangements.

Essential members of the research team have been our link staff: Hilary Cain, Mary Fisher and Trixie Taylor. Lindsey Bernardo in the early part of the study, and later Mary Gage, have provided valuable administrative and secretarial support. We would like to express our appreciation to all of them. There were no weak links in the chain.

All our data processing and computer work was undertaken by Social and Community Planning Research. We have been particularly grateful to Steve Elder for his patience with our endless requests and his skill in handling our complicated data set.

Professor Roy Parker as chairman of our advisory committee and Stephen P. Rashid, chairman of our Black Issues Advisory Group, were very helpful and we would to thank them and the members of these committees for their interest and suggestions.

Finally, we wish to thank British Agencies for Adoption & Fostering for sponsoring the project and Christine Hammond in particular for her help and advice. The financial support of the DHSS made the study possible and we have been specially grateful to Carolyn Davies for her patient encouragement and confidence in us. At times when we have been almost overwhelmed by the size and complexity of the task, this helped us to keep going.

Jane Rowe
Marion Hundleby
Louise Garnett

The full report of this research project, Child care placements: patterns and outcomes, *including appendices with detailed statistics, information on the research and the questionnaires used, is available from BAAF, details on request.*

Contents

Note on the advisory committees

Three advisory committees/groups helped with various aspects of the project. The first grew out of the original pilot working party. It was chaired by Professor Roy Parker and was composed of researchers or those with special interest in research. In the early stages of the project, this committee provided much help and advice on sources of information and some of the methodological problems we were encountering. Later it proved rather difficult to get the group together but we had continuing contact with individual members as we followed through their leads and advice.

A crucial element in achieving co-operation and keeping up the momentum of the project was a Steering Group made up of one or two representatives from each of the six participating authorities. The Group met regularly throughout the project, worked hard and harmoniously and was a source of real strength and support.

We called together the third advisory committee when we realised that we had potentially important data about black children in care. We felt the need for advice on practical issues such as how to deal with small sub-groups which needed to be amalgamated for analysis and, more importantly, we wanted help in interpreting our findings. This proved even more useful than expected because, as Chapter 12 shows, our findings about black children in care were rather different from expectation. The group was chaired by Stephen P. Rashid, Lecturer in Social Work at the University of East Anglia. Its members were black social workers and administrators from the four authorities in the project which had a substantial number of black children in care.

Because it has been agreed that the six authorities will not be identified, we are not listing the members of these committees.

1 About the project:
Its background, evolution, aims,
experience and methodology

The roots of this study go back to the early 1980s when we were analysing the data from our study of long-term foster care.[1] It was a surprise to discover that five out of every six of the children had been less than five years old when they joined their foster family. Since we knew that a lot of school aged children were placed for long-term fostering, our findings suggested that many of the placements of older children must have broken down. But when we looked for up-to-date national figures on fostering outcomes to test out this supposition, we found that none existed. This deficiency seemed particularly serious because the move was in full swing toward closing residential establishments and placing more children in foster homes in the community. It seemed important to try to find out how well current foster placements were succeeding in meeting children's needs and to develop a basic monitoring system that authorities could easily maintain.

British Agencies for Adoption and Fostering offered strong support for these ideas and officials at the Department of Health and Social Security were also interested. However, tentative ideas about a major study of foster care had soon to be abandoned in face of both practical and methodological problems. No one knew how many children were being placed, in what sort of foster homes or how long the placements were lasting. Moreover, there was no clear professional agreement about what constituted either a fostering 'breakdown' or a successful outcome. The DHSS therefore agreed to fund 18 months of pilot work which developed into the Child Care Placement Outcomes Project.

The pilot work
The pilot work was done during 1984-5 in 20 local authorities which volunteered to cooperate. The main purpose was to develop, test and revise questionnaires to be used in collecting information from social workers at the beginning and end of foster placements. Using the

questionnaires enabled us to try out the systems for notifying movements of children in care. Some trial analysis was also undertaken.

Another important aspect was an attempt by a specially constituted working party to find an agreed terminology and develop a rating scale for fostering outcomes. In spite of the working party's best efforts, it proved impossible to develop a satisfactory rating scale. Terminology also proved elusive, but the experience was invaluable in highlighting the complexity of the issues. It also provided the basis for evaluating a number of small scale local studies of fostering breakdown which became available at about this time.[2] Without the extensive pilot work and the wide consultation, the survey we are reporting here would have been very different and almost certainly less successful.

The lessons learned during those 18 months shaped the present project in four ways:

Extension from fostering to all child care placements
The original plan to limit enquiries to the outcome of foster placements was extended to include all in-care placements. Social workers argued strongly for this extension because information was needed on all types of placement and also because fostering outcomes can only be properly evaluated if they are compared with outcomes from residential and 'home on trial' placements. The decision to extend inevitably had a profound effect on the scale and complexity of the study even though there was never any expectation that other types of placement would be explored as thoroughly as foster care.

Need for descriptive information about participating authorities
It became clear that if any real sense was to be made of differences between local authorities in the outcomes of their child care placements, we would need to know something about authorities' policies and the structure and organisation of their services. We were particularly interested to know whether having specialist fostering staff had any noticeable effect on outcome of fostering placements since this has been an important and contentious issue. The project was therefore designed to include a descriptive element that would underpin and inform the statistical work.

Limitations on the data that could be obtained
The pilot work uncovered a remarkably high level of interest among managers and practitioners and an unexpected but most welcome willingness to complete questionnaires. However, it was also quite evident that busy social workers could not take time to look up information in files. We realised that if we wanted to achieve a high response rate over an extended period, we would have to forfeit some items of information that might not be immediately to hand, such as the date of admission to care or the number of previous admissions.

We therefore made a decision that we would ask only for information which social workers usually carry in their heads and would omit questions about the past, such as previous admissions and placements. This had excellent results in achieving co-operation from field workers, but it meant some loss of information and one or two frustrating gaps in our data. Given the scale of our survey and our slender staffing resources, we still think the decision was right, but the disadvantages have to be acknowledged. The most serious loss is not knowing how long children moving into the project had already been in care.

Administrative difficulties
The lessons learned during the pilot brought home to us the scale of effort required to establish and maintain a monitoring study and the frailty of existing social services' statistical and information systems. We realised that, in addition to the liaison work which would be undertaken by the researchers, we would have to have part-time project staff based in or near our participating authorities to ensure that data collection would continue smoothly.

Aims and limitations
When the project was launched in the autumn of 1984 it had three main aims:

To provide basic information on the numbers and characteristics of children going into various types of placement and the outcome of these placements. Fostering, adoption, residential care and placements 'home on trial' would all be included. We hoped to build a data base that would be of immediate use and interest and might also provide a firm platform for further studies.

To investigate the possible links between placement outcomes and

9

the organisation of services, through a parallel descriptive study. Because of the magnitude of this task, we would only attempt to trace these links in relation to the fostering service which was still the central focus of the study.

To test and demonstrate the viability, strengths and weaknesses of a monitoring system. We hoped to develop a system that could become a routine part of an authority's work and become increasingly valuable as it was maintained over a period. We also aimed to use project experience to develop some kind of 'workbook' that would be of assistance to middle managers and specialist staff who need to monitor placements but lack research experience and do not have easy access to the small, hard-pressed research and information units that are all most social services departments can provide.

Limitations were imposed by the very small size of the project's staff – one full-time and one part-time researcher, three locally based and very part-time workers and a part-time secretary/administrator. During the course of the project, funds were obtained to employ a research assistant – first part-time and later nearly full-time.

However, the main limitation on our project is its reliance on information provided by social workers. To get a rounded picture it would be necessary to seek the views of the children and young people in care, their parents and their care-givers. One would also need details of the composition and experience of foster families and the regimes of residential establishments. Not only did we lack the resources to obtain and analyse data from this range of respondents, we also realised that it would be entirely impractical to suppose that hard-pressed social services departments could maintain this kind of monitoring service.

So, sadly but quite deliberately, we limited this study to a broad but shallow survey. We planned to investigate what is going on but knew that we could not discover the reasons. Thus we set out to try to answer 'what' questions such as: 'What sort of children? What sort of placements? How long? What happened next?' We did not attempt to ask why, acknowledging that the 'why' questions and answers would have to come later.

The design of the project

A major factor in the design of this survey was the need to gather information about the outcome of long-stay placements. It would have been simplest to pick a cohort of new placements and study them for the duration of the project. But if we had done only this, we would still be none the wiser about how long-lasting placements turn out. Is it true, for instance, that many long-term foster homes break down when the children are in their teens? Are many young people being pushed into foster homes because the residential establishments in which they have been living are closing down? We wanted to get at least some answers to questions like these and so the project was designed to collect information about all placement starts and all placement endings during a two year period in six local authorities from April 1985 to March 1987. This meant that we would have information about admissions, discharges, re-admissions and moves between placements. Although we would not learn anything about children in settled, long-term placements who neither came, went nor moved during the project, we would build up a picture of the turnover of children in care to counterbalance the rather static impression which one gets from the DHSS annual statistics.

Clearly there are disadvantages as well as benefits in a sample of this type. It is a disadvantage to know nothing of the children who 'stay put' in the care of project authorities. It would have been advantageous to have had a third year of data collection because this would have given us endings to most of the placements made during the first year. (Only about 12 per cent of placements are planned to last for more than two years.) However, the most serious problem has been the complexity of the project data in terms of analysis and the difficulty of presenting the findings clearly and succinctly.

In spite of these disadvantages, we can say that if our sample is untidy and our data complex, they are also rich. It may be potentially confusing to be able to look both forward and backward. Using different segments of the data to explore different issues has its hazards. But we are fortunate in not being bound by the confines of either a cohort study or an entirely retrospective study. Provided that we and the reader can hold on to the definitions and thread our way carefully through the complexities, we can have something of the best of both worlds.

The six authorities
Selecting the six authorities proved relatively easy. We started with three that had taken part in the pilot and approached others to achieve

a balance. We wanted different types and sizes of authority, a wide geographical spread, inclusion of those using specialist foster care workers and those employing only generic staff. We also sought a balance of authorities with high and low boarding-out rates. We were about to settle for five when a sixth authority approached us expressing interest in participating. We gladly agreed because they provided useful balance and breadth and they joined in half way through the first year of data collection. So for this authority our data only cover 18 months.

Our authorities are: a large, northern city, hereafter referred to as City; a much smaller, neighbouring metropolitan district, referred to as District; a partly industrialised midlands county (Midshire); a home county (County) and two London boroughs (North Thames and South Thames). No six authorities can be considered to provide a really satisfactory national sample, but we believe that our authorities offer a reasonably balanced national picture.

The system
The system used for data collection was developed during the pilot work. It was based on the existing arrangements which almost all departments have for social workers to notify the administration of admissions, discharges and moves of children in care. These movement sheets triggered the dispatch of the appropriate project questionnaires to the social worker of the child involved. This method had the dual advantage of not relying on social workers remembering to notify the project and enabling administrative staff in the department and/or the project to keep track of questionnaires and chase them up when necessary.

Defining placement
Defining what we meant by placement required attention and discussion with the project steering group. From the start, it was decided to exclude: holidays from boarding school, holidays with parents and relatives, trial visits to prospective foster or adoptive parents and relief placements of disabled children cared for under Mental Health legislation. It also became clear almost immediately that it was impractical to include moves of emancipated teenagers making their own arrangements to live with friends. Our questionnaires were not devised with this sort of move in mind. For much the same

reasons we did not consider absconding to be a move, provided that the child returned to the same establishment. Apart from these exclusions, all placements of children in care or under place of safety orders were to be included in the survey.

The descriptive study

The descriptive study of the six authorities was carried out separately from the data collection but in parallel. The part-time research worker has taken responsibility for both the fieldwork and the report on this part of the study. She made a number of visits to each authority. Useful information was also obtained from a literature scan of studies and statistics which compare and/or describe local authorities.

The central focus of the enquiry was the foster care service but inevitably it was necessary to widen this in order to make sense of fostering developments, or lack of them. Preventive services and residential provision both strongly affect foster care needs and numbers. Less obvious, but equally powerful, are the influences of local traditions and expectations and the socio-economic background against which services are being provided.

The fieldwork experience

Considering the pressures under which most social workers in our project authorities were working, their willingness to co-operate was remarkable. It was perhaps helped by their finding that completing our questionnaires was often quite helpful because it offered an opportunity to review plans for the child and how they had worked out. A few individuals were constitutionally allergic to completing forms and we had a minority of those we termed 'delinquents' who had to be constantly reminded and chased up. Sometimes when a backlog had built up or a social worker was burdened with a string of questionnaires on a large family of children or a youngster who had a series of rapid moves, we found the best solution was to visit the office and lend a hand. Most generic social workers only had to complete questionnaires rather occasionally. For them, the problem was that they never became very familiar with them. But social workers with a big child care caseload found our questionnaires on their desks quite frequently and could sometimes be faced with a pile of them which must have been quite daunting.

All the completed questionnaires (about 25,000 by the end) were checked by project staff as they came in. We agreed on what were the crucial questions, and if answers to these were missing or ambiguous, we telephoned for clarification. This process was an essential step in obtaining accurate, usable information because there were a good many errors . The checking process also enabled us to keep track of every child who entered the project. In this way we could chase missing data as we went along.

Administrative staff were for the most part very helpful, interested and conscientious. But the difficulties under which they work and the general frailty of social services administrative systems were manifested many times. One of the problems about a monitoring system is that it has to be maintained in areas or divisions as well as by an authority's central administration. If even one area cannot cope for a while, the validity of the whole exercise may be in jeopardy. None of the six project authorities was able to manage its agreed part of the project work without additional input from us, though the amount of help needed varied greatly.

Three of our authorities had computerised systems and a fourth was installing computers as our project was coming to an end. We used these systems to check our data and found them extremely helpful but they were not always up to date and in any case could provide only limited information. They do not include any evaluation of placement outcome.

Whereas we had hoped to encourage at least some of our six authorities to continue the monitoring after the project was over, we found ourselves increasingly concerned about their ability to maintain the system, check and chase the questionnaires and then find staff with the time and experience to process the data and do the analysis. In the end, none of the six felt able to continue on their own although two of them would have very much liked to do so.

Questions of validity
There are four main issues concerning the validity of the survey findings: the sample, missing data, problems and ambiguities arising from the questionnaires, and reliance on social workers' perceptions.

The sample
We believe that our authorities are as representative as any six are likely to be. Our one concern has been the possible distortion caused by

the size of City which accounts for one third of the sample. If there are peculiarities in City's policy or practice that might affect our overall findings, we draw attention to these in the chapters which follow.

Because we included all admissions to care, discharges and moves, there is no problem of sampling bias. The numbers involved are large – a total of 5868 children who between them experienced over 10,000 placements. This means that, when looking at the whole data set, there is usually no problem about the size of subgroups. However, when comparisons need to be made between the six authorities, or between age groups, types of placement or ethnic groups, then numbers sometimes become too small for reliable conclusions to be drawn. This has limited comparison between authorities on certain topics and has precluded some types of analysis, but constraints on time and resources would in any case have made it difficult to take the analysis any further.

Missing data

There were two ways in which we may have lost data. The first loss might come from social workers failing to return questionnaires. We are confident that, after considerable effort, we collected at least 95 per cent of the questionnaires sent out, though a few were incomplete.

A more worrying aspect was whether we were picking up news of all admissions, moves and discharges. The latter were particularly problematic because there always seems to be less attention paid to discharges than admissions.[3]

When the collection of data was completed, we found that we did indeed have considerably more placement starts than placement ends. We decided to check up on all placements which appeared to have exceeded their expected length by more than eight weeks except those which had started in the last three months of the project. There were 471 of these overstayers. Our enquiries revealed that 301 (64%) of the children were still in the same placement, 87 (18%) had moved and 83 (18%) had been discharged. They were a random group with some from each authority and with all age groups and types of placement represented.

By the time we had chased up this information, it was too late to send out more questionnaires or alter our data set on the computer. We considered making some adjustments to the figures in this report but concluded that it would only be confusing for us and for readers and the numbers involved are too small to make significant differences to our findings.

In a perfect world, our figures for admissions would tally exactly with those in the DHSS annual return. In fact, ours are slightly lower. It appears to be generally accepted that the DHSS returns are not entirely accurate and that they are more inclined to overcount than undercount because of complications over legal care episodes. We have no way of knowing the extent to which this may be occurring. However, we feel sure that we have not missed many children who remained in care for a period or moved around in the system. We think we may not have been notified of some very brief admissions (for example, children brought into care by night duty teams or the police and returned home almost immediately). No survey which has to rely on hundreds of individuals and involves thousands of cases can hope for total accuracy but we are confident that our data provide a true reflection of the movements of children in care.

Problems and ambiguities arising from the questionnaires
The scale of the survey meant that all the answers had to be pre-coded and this inevitably required respondents to categorise their plans, expectations and opinions even when, in reality, these may still have been rather fluid.

The questionnaires were re-drafted many times during and after the pilot work. It proved remarkably difficult to focus the questions so that they covered almost all eventualities, were unambiguous and as short as possible. The decision to extend the survey beyond foster care required a number of additions to the questionnaire which were made after the pilot work was completed and were therefore inadequately tested. Categories of residential establishment proved particularly hard to define because of the wide variety in size, usage and nomenclature.

For the most part, the questionnaires proved very satisfactory as regards data collection but somewhat less so when it came to analysis. In the light of our experience, we plan further improvements for inclusion in the monitoring 'workbook' which we hope to make available.

The first problem that emerged during analysis was that there are evident ambiguities in responses to questions about social worker choice and the appropriateness of the placements. Perhaps the issues were too complex to deal with in a postal questionnaire. Fortunately, they were matters of interest rather than central concern. Rather more serious has been our growing realisation that we should not place too much reliance on social workers' responses to the question on whether the circumstances of the placement ending were planned or unplanned. We tried to make it clear that the question did not refer to the way the move or discharge was carried out but to whether it was part of the plan for the child. But as the analysis progressed, it became clear that people had sometimes coded a move as planned when their answers to other questions made it seem certain that it was not what had been intended and hoped for.

An obvious example is a placement which was coded as a planned move, but the aim had been 'care and upbringing' with an expected length of 'over five years' and it ended in less than six months with the child's move to a residential establishment. Instances like this were relatively few in number, but we feel it best to use the 'planned' figures with great caution. When 'unplanned' is coded, we think it is almost always correct but our figures are certainly an undercount. In the tables in this report, the planned/unplanned distinction has been dropped.

The only other question which proved troublesomely ambiguous was whether the placement had lasted as long as the child needed it. The first two responses 'Lasted as long as needed' and 'Did not last as long as needed' are perfectly straightforward. But we felt we had to make allowance for situations where social workers considered that the placement had gone on too long. It transpired that the 'too long' coding was used for cases where it was felt that the child should never have been placed at all, for placements which ended as planned but after an extended time and for cases where the placement was not very satisfactory and the child should have left sooner. Thus for some parts of the analysis it has been necessary to omit the 'lasted too long' cases.

In re-designing the questionnaires to accommodate residential placements, we wanted to distinguish between different types of establishment. Unfortunately, in an effort to avoid repetition and keep the questionnaires short and simple, we made this distinction only on the start of placement questionnaire. The one for the end of the placement puts all residential care together. It was only when we came to do the final analysis that we realised that we would not have information on the type of residential establishment for the ends of those placements which began before the project started. If residential care had been included in our pilot work, the gap would have been identified during the pilot analysis.

Reliance on social workers' perceptions
Some reference has already been made to the limitations imposed by having only the social workers' views but the difference between hard and soft data must also be borne in mind. When we are dealing with facts such as age or length of placement we are on firm ground. Less tangible matters such as the child's behaviour or intelligence are inevitably affected both by how well the child is known and also by individual perceptions. When it comes to opinions such as whether the placement was helpful, then inevitably we are dealing with 'soft' data requiring considerable caution in interpretation.

Analysis
By the time we came to analysing the data, new interests had emerged which affected the focus of the analysis. Studies by the Dartington Social Research Units[4] and by Thorpe[5] highlighted patterns in children's length of stay in care and the leaving care curve. There had been increasing concern, especially in the black community, about the number of black children in care. Place of safety orders and the use of compulsory powers have been under scrutiny and sometimes under attack. We realised that our data would sometimes enable us to fill gaps in information or provide useful comparisons on topics which we had not anticipated would be of particular interest. Thus we felt it necessary to consider care episodes as well as individual placements, to pay special attention to some legal aspects and to make maximum use of our data on children from ethnic minorities. Because we started with a rather fluid structure, it was possible to adapt and develop the data to meet these additional demands. But there were considerable methodological problems, because we had not always got the data in a convenient form. The appointment of a research assistant with a statistical background was essential and the project could not have been completed without her.

It was planned from the start that the data processing and computer work would be undertaken on our behalf by Social and Community Planning Research. This had the enormous advantage of having an experienced data processor to handle our complex problems and use a variety of programmes according to our needs. It had the serious disadvantage that we had no direct access to the data and had to order the tables we needed and then wait for them to come. Because we needed to be able to look at and compare so many sub-sets of data (age groups, ethnic groups, types of placement and authorities), we required huge numbers of tables and the ordering, checking and indexing was itself a time-consuming task.

As the analysis progressed, we became increasingly aware of the need to set each piece of information in context in order to avoid misleading interpretations. This was particularly important when making comparisons between authorities and at this stage the descriptive data which we had collected became invaluable.

Ever since the publication of Packman's *Child care needs and numbers,*[6] researchers and administrators have sought to understand and account for major differences between authorities in the proportions of children admitted to care, the type of care provided, and the financial resources allocated to child care services. Our findings, too, show up many differences between the policies and practices of social services departments and the way in which they make provision for children in care. However, when we looked at outcomes, we were surprised to find what appeared to be a quite remarkable degree of similarity between our six authorities.

For a long time we found this extremely perplexing. Gradually, as the analysis progressed, we realised that overall figures can mask considerable differences between sub-groups which, when amalgamated, more or less cancel each other out and produce a rather spurious uniformity. Secondly, differences between authorities in the characteristics of both children and placements may mean that one is not really comparing like with like. We became increasingly aware of the need for extreme caution when making comparisons.

We also began to understand more of the interaction of placement policies and placement outcomes. Although we are not in a position to measure or evaluate these interactions, we believe it is important for policy makers, managers and social workers to appreciate their importance in order to avoid drawing false conclusions about what is going on in their authority.

For example, if an authority devotes many resources to keeping children and young people out of care, most of those who are admitted are likely to have serious problems and many of them are likely to remain in care for a considerable time. Care episodes may therefore be of above average length thus causing anxiety about possible drift and lack of planning. Again, if an authority pursues an adventurous fostering and adoption policy and tries to 'push out the frontiers' by placing more older, disturbed and disabled children, then fostering costs will go up and the proportion of breakdowns is likely to increase. Above average skill will be required to achieve outcomes that appear to be no more successful than those achieved by authorities with lower standards of practice but which 'play safe' in their foster care and adoption work.

In the long run, the most important lesson to be learned from this project may be the way in which the dangers and difficulties of making comparisons have been highlighted by our findings and through our efforts to understand them properly. We hope that our experience will help others to avoid drawing false conclusions from any monitoring or research studies which they undertake in future.

References

1   Rowe J, Cain H, Hundleby M and Keane A *Long term foster care* Batsford Academic/ BAAF, 1984.

2   Rowe J 'Interpreting breakdown rates' *Adoption & Fostering* 11 1 1984.

3   Fisher M, Marsh P, Phillips D and Sainsbury E *In and out of care* Batsford Academic/BAAF, 1986.

4   Millham S et al *Place of Safety Orders* Report to the DHSS, 1984; *Predicting children's length of stay in care and the relevance of family links* Report to the DHSS, 1984.

5   Thorpe D 'Career patterns in child care – implications for the service' *British Journal of Social Work* 18 2, 1987.

6   Packman J *Child care needs and numbers* Allen & Unwin, 1968.

2 An overview of the project authorities

During the course of the research we found ourselves comparing and contrasting the six participating authorities in a number of ways and for various reasons. Of primary importance was the need to place our statistical data in their context. However, it was also a matter of considerable interest to see how six rather different departments found solutions to a range of problems which were broadly similar. For example, all our authorities were having to make decisions about the most appropriate way to meet the needs of children in their care, all were grappling with a shortage of resources in the face of ever-increasing demand, and all were operating within the same legal framework. Yet at times it was very hard to remember these common threads as the differences always seemed to loom larger than the similarities. As anyone who is familiar with social services will know, differences within departments are often very great, too. It was fascinating to see how local tradition and the influence of key people in the organisation could be far more potent than organisational edicts imposed from above.

As well as acknowledging the characteristics of each department and trying to obtain some insight into their policies and resources, we were also faced with the problem of change during the two years of our fieldwork. Two of our authorities, County and North Thames, experienced a total re-organisation in this period and Midshire was still feeling the effects of a previous re-organisation. North Thames re-organised relatively soon after our project began and had completed their changes by the end of our first year, but County did not alter its way of working until three months before our fieldwork finished. Therefore, the only sensible course of action seemed to be to describe structures as they were for the majority of the fieldwork period, which means that for County the information refers to their previous system.

It is surprisingly difficult to become familiar with six social services departments and in order to make the task manageable it has been necessary to concentrate on matters which are clearly defined and documented. In addition, efforts have been made to add some local flavour through the perceptions of the staff we interviewed. To set the scene, we start by looking at size and population.

Size and population

Although the geographical size of an authority has a number of implications for its structure, a useful picture only really begins to emerge when this is considered alongside population. Figures which show that the area per 1000 of the population is over fifty times greater in Midshire than in North Thames make one realise the very different (although equally complex) dilemmas which departments face when providing a service.

Age distribution is important in the provision of social services and we wanted to see whether there were any major differences between our authorities in this respect. We found that whereas the density of population varies considerably, the proportion of pre-school children in the population is very similar across the six. This consistency alters slightly when a comparison is made for the five to 18 age group. Although four of the authorities are again very similar, the two London boroughs both have three per cent to four per cent fewer young people of this age.

The differences in population size and socio-economic characteristics are, of course, carried through into the numbers and proportions of children in care which are set out in the tables below.

Table 2.1

Population of project authorities in 1985 (in thousands)

City	District	Midshire	County	N. Thames	S. Thames
743	252	564	978	168	278

Staffing levels

Except for Midshire and County, which were fractionally better off for social workers, our authorities were slightly less well staffed than comparable departments, as shown in social services statistics. With the exception of City, the administrative staffing levels were also slightly lower than average, but, again, differences were only slight.

In the brief pen portraits which follow, we have not attempted to

Table 2.2

Number of children in care and number of children in care per 1000 of the population under 18. Source DHSS statistics 1985

City	District	Midshire	County	N.Thames	S.Thames
1494	286	799	883	655*	618
8.81	4.40	5.73	3.70	19.00**	11.20

obtained direct – DHSS figures not available.
**our calculation – DHSS figures not available.*

report methodically because there would be much tedious repetition. Instead we have tried to highlight the most interesting aspects of each authority's services, making comparisons only when these seem particularly pertinent.

City

Perhaps the most notable characteristic of City is its size. It covers a vast area of Northern England and comprises several small towns together with an urban core and rural hinterland. As we travelled from area to area we were constantly amazed by the contrasts. Area offices varied from Victorian Town Halls, tatty but still reminiscent of the grandeur of a former age with stained glass windows and tiled floors, to offices on post-war estates with boarded up windows and graffiti-covered outer walls.

Despite the considerable area covered by City and the range of local identities encompassed, the authority is one of the most centralised of the six we studied. It was described by members of staff as having a 'traditional' approach, more likely to modify existing resources than to make fundamental alterations in provision or organisation. An example of this is found in City's residential care for children. Unlike many other authorities, City has not sanctioned a drastic policy of closing homes; instead, it has converted some of its family group homes to accommodate mentally handicapped adults, and made internal changes to other homes which are still used for children so as to improve their staff/child ratio. Although some closures have been made, the overall picture is one of rationalisation rather than decimation and the heavy investment in residential care, for which this authority is well-known, still remains.

23

Some of City's residential homes are unusually large – 100 places, for example, in one – but the multi-functional nature of the larger establishments goes some way to offset their scale because they contain a number of separate units. By and large, vacancies (in particular those for short-term places), are handled via the central office and all residential resources are authority-wide. We were told that if time permits or if a long-term placement is needed, social workers frequently make an informal approach to the head of home first, but, even so, this arrangement differs from most of our other authorities where some, if not the majority of establishments, are local resources 'owned' by an area.

We were interested to find out about preventive work in all the project authorities, as an understanding of policies and practice in this field enables one to make better sense of data relating to children in care. The picture that emerged from City was not altogether encouraging, although this authority does provide a generous number of nursery places which social workers said were relatively easy to obtain. A scheme whereby Home Helps could assist families whose children were at risk of admission to care was beginning in some areas as our fieldwork drew to a close. Enthusiasm was expressed for this scheme and also for Family Centres, a resource which City does not have at present. Underlying many of the comments was a frustration about lack of money to try anything new and imaginative. Section 1 money was said to be scarce, and the amount available to areas very low. Perhaps this was because the amount was set over a decade ago and has remained unchanged. In comparison with our London boroughs, the proportion of ethnic minority families in City is rather small. However, because it is such a very large authority, the actual number of black families living in City is quite large. The 1981 Census reported that nearly 28,000 household heads were born in New Commonwealth countries or Pakistan. Half were from India or Pakistan. While our project was in progress, City's social services department was becoming increasingly concerned about Black issues.

District

Compared with City, District, which is only about half an hour's drive away, seems diminutive and sparsely populated. In fact, it is one of the larger Metropolitan Districts in terms of geographical size but it has a relatively low number of inhabitants. District consists of an industrial town surrounded by modern estates, villages and open countryside. The workforce has traditionally been employed in coal-mining and metal manufacture, but since the 1960s, unemployment has risen steeply and many workers now find it necessary to travel to a nearby city in order to obtain employment. Although changing work patterns must have altered the way of life for many families, there is still a strong sense of community. Of our six authorities, District is probably the most traditional and least varied culturally, with a less mobile population than the other five and the presence of extended family to act as a buffer between the public and services provided by the state.

Whether the availability of community help was the cause or the effect of the paucity of provision in District can only be speculated upon, but we noted that social services were frequently more conspicuous by their absence than their presence. For example, the department has no day nurseries, provides no registered child minders, has no family centres and was only just beginning to establish an emergency duty team as our fieldwork was concluded. It is not appropriate to make judgements about whether certain services and facilities 'should' be available. It may be that District's population manages to provide on a self-help basis the resources that many other departments see as their responsibility. However, social work staff frequently spoke of the lack of preventive services for children and expressed the hope that our research would strengthen their case for improved resources. During our study, some additions to the preventive services were made. A day fostering scheme to keep children out of care was started and Family Aides were also used for this purpose. The availability of Section 1 money was also increased in order to pay relatives caring for a child without the need for admission to care.

There were many changes in District's child care policy and practice during this period and much was achieved, though some changes were too recent to be reflected in the study figures. A central family care unit for all adoption work and for foster family recruitment and preparation had been set up just before our project started. By the spring of 1987 it was beginning to develop foster care resources for adolescents. Like City, District is by tradition a heavy user of residential resources for children's care, but since the early 1980s occupancy rates have decreased dramatically. This has led to a number of home closures and a policy of improving staff/child ratios. The department is also moving towards more specialised use of certain homes, for example with emphasis on preparation for foster care or preparation for independent living.

Although in some ways District seems limited in what it has to offer both to staff and clients, there are some benefits related to its size. The combination of few area offices, a small central management team and considerable area autonomy does enable people to get things done.

Midshire

Midshire is geographically the largest of all the participating authorities, but is more sparsely populated than its counterpart, County. In view of its size, it is hardly surprising that it comprises a whole range of small towns and villages, a new town and a county town large enough to have been an authority in its own right before local government re-organisation. Midshire, unlike District, has an increasingly significant service sector, the major growth areas being transport and communication, distribution, insurance, banking and professional and scientific services. Since the 1950s, Midshire has accommodated a substantial number of migrants from other parts of the British Isles, in particular Scotland, who have been attracted by the employment and housing available in the county. Although Midshire is regionally part of the East Midlands, it has shared in the increasing affluence of the South of England and enjoys reasonable access to London by road and rail. The rural areas of the authority are in places extremely wealthy with more than a sprinkling of stately homes and picturesque thatched cottages.

In addition to socio-economic changes, a prolonged re-organisation seems to have played a large part in this authority's recent history and, as in other places, has left its scars. We were sometimes struck by the contrast between, on the one hand, the young and dynamic management team who were formally spearheading the work of the department, and the 'old stayers', many of whom were in lowly positions in the hierarchy but who had a wealth of knowledge going back for years and who made a major contribution to holding the service together. In common with our other five authorities, Midshire lacked efficient information systems across the department and it could be frustrating to find that full and helpful information available from one division was completely absent in others.

In the early 1980s, Midshire made major changes in the allocation of resources, closed residential establishments which at that time were under-used and developed children's centres. It was decided that demand did not justify inclusion of a residential element in these centres. Unfortunately, soon after there was an unexpected and rapid upturn in the numbers requiring residential care and this created many pressures and problems as well as improvements in service to families. Although the number of children in care has declined, the problem of lack of choice seemed particularly acute in Midshire. The remaining residential homes were bursting at the seams for most of our fieldwork period. The staff dealing with fostering also felt the effect of this as the pressure on foster home places mounted. Another result was the development of an assisted lodgings scheme which now plays a considerable part in Midshire's provision for its older adolescents.

We were able to look at a few interesting local schemes, among them a 'Carers Scheme' in one division which aims to prevent admission to care. The scheme is funded out of the boarding-out budget and tasks are written into a contract agreed by the department, the family and the carer. A typical example of the help a carer may give is teaching parenting skills to clients in the carer's home. Social workers described it as 'almost like an extended family', since it gave vital support through a period of crisis. Family carers are registered under the dual system of childminders and foster parents to enable the child to stay overnight, if necessary. Initially it was envisaged that the scheme would recruit separately but childminders heard about it through the networks and have been the main source of applicants. Although the target group tends to be the under-fives, the scheme was set up with a view to providing flexible but time-limited help to any child who needs it, and older children have also been recipients. Parents are not asked to make a financial contribution as it was thought that redeeming the money would probably be more costly than the revenue produced. As with so many areas of social work, and in particular preventive services, defining and measuring 'success' is extremely difficult. Nevertheless, those who managed the scheme needed no convincing of its merits.

County
Although County is only about two-thirds the size of Midshire in area, its population is nearly twice as large. In terms of population it was the

largest of all our project authorities. Situated to the north of London it is strategically well placed in terms of the motorway network and accessible airports. Train links to London are fast and frequent. During our fieldwork period there was a dramatic increase in house and land prices which were already high. Whereas in Midshire people were likely both to live and to work within the county, and indeed many people had been attracted by the availability of work and housing, County has a large commuter population. Every morning thousands of people travel into London to work but can enjoy the picturesque villages and rural areas of County in their free time. As house prices soared, County faced difficulties in recruiting staff because re-location could prove prohibitively expensive to people wishing to move there from other parts of the country.

Three months before the end of our fieldwork period, County's social services underwent a total restructuring. Its nine divisions were re-organised into four, each of which is co-terminous with a Health Authority. In effect, much of the power which was formerly based at the authority's headquarters was re-located further down the structure, thus providing a service that could be more self-sufficient and responsive to need on a local basis. Our research was therefore conducted in a climate of considerable uncertainty. For the purposes of this profile, it is only possible to consider the structure as it was until the end of 1986.

Inevitably with an authority of this size, there are significant differences between the service needs of each of the divisions, and even under the old structure it was possible for areas to exercise autonomy in deciding how to use posts or whether to develop small projects. It seems a tradition in County to respond imaginatively to service needs and it was interesting to learn about the various schemes which were in operation. We found that preventive services were well-developed for children of all ages, but particularly for the under-fives. Nine establishments were being used as family centres, eight of which had originally been built as day nurseries. These functioned on a daily basis and provided care, advice and supervision for children and their parents. Most of their work was structured, with an emphasis on assessment. An additional service for families was that of the family help or family aide. The original job description defined the task as: 'to work with members of families where there is difficulty in planning, managing and carrying out everyday tasks such as budgeting, shopping, caring for children and management of the home. The objective is to teach persons to do such things so that the family can function to the best of its ability.'

This scheme bears a certain similarity to others in Midshire, District and City, but extends beyond children to other client groups, for example the mentally handicapped and the elderly.

Another scheme which we heard about in County was 'guesting'. It seems to be unique to this authority and involves the accommodation of children in local residential homes for up to 72 hours. The child remains the responsibility of the parents but they agree in writing to the department caring for the child and taking decisions should an emergency arise. Guesting allows for a cooling-off period during a family crisis and it can in some ways be likened to visits to the extended family.

Not all the preventive schemes in County are directed towards the needs of younger children. 'Homelink' is another service which is aimed at containing the sudden 'blow-up', this time by providing overnight accommodation for teenagers with approved families.

We found that the various schemes tended to be small and not used equally by all the areas. Somehow traditions had built up about strategies for certain situations and what seemed the obvious next step to one team would perhaps be almost unknown to another. However, County appears well-disposed to try various ways of solving its problems.

In common with all our non-London authorities, County has only a small ethnic minority population. During the project, attempts were being made to scrutinise service delivery for this section of the population in order to ensure that they received the appropriate range of resources. Mainly, however, County is dealing with a population which is white, geographically mobile, mostly employed and relatively affluent.

North Thames

By any standard, North Thames is geographically tiny. Measuring just three miles by five miles, it is the smallest and most densely populated of our project authorities, a vibrant microcosm of London life: ethnically very mixed, historically and culturally rich, and containing extreme examples of affluence and poverty. Seventy per cent of the housing stock in North Thames is owned either by housing associations or the local authority. Alongside the recently gentrified streets of owner-occupied property, long-established communities remain in council or housing association property, and the social services department has endeavoured to stay closely in touch with these local networks. This authority enjoys a high media profile, being an example of the 'loony left' as far as much of the national and regional press is concerned, and often castigated by them. Strong commitment to a generic and locally based social work service is evident throughout the department and the few specialist posts are purely advisory.

Working with North Thames posed a major challenge for our research team. Not only did their re-organisation coincide with our fieldwork period, but we also found ourselves dealing with a department which had virtually no tradition of collecting information about its work. This lack of data even extended to the submission of statistics to government departments.

During our two years of fieldwork, the department underwent many changes. The biggest of these was the devolution from ten area offices into a large number of local 'patch' offices, but other changes, such as the policy to close out-of-borough resources continued alongside the creation of a 'patch' system. We were aware of two processes at work. On the one hand, efforts were made to respond as appropriately and effectively as possible to local need and this was likely to increase differences in provision from one area to another. On the other hand, it was acknowledged that in some respects greater standardisation was necessary. One result of this was the development of the department's first, written child care policy document to provide guidance for staff working with children and families.

Residential provision for children in care in North Thames was also in a somewhat 'fluid' state. Several out-of-borough homes were closed around the time of our fieldwork and just before. Resources are very unevenly distributed throughout the borough, which means that some local offices have far more establishments on their patch than others. The aim was to close resources outside the borough and to reduce numbers accommodated in the private and voluntary sectors. Plans were also afoot to designate a couple of units for preparing children in need of family placement. However, North Thames has been subject to very serious financial cutbacks, and plans outlined to us at the beginning of our research may have been delayed or scrapped due to lack of resources.

For a department that seems very aware of its clients' needs and sympathetic to them, North Thames appeared surprisingly unprogressive in some respects. For example, there were no family centres when our project started and recruitment of black staff and of substitute families from ethnic minorities was less than might be expected given the department's level of racial awareness and its commitment to equal opportunities. Nevertheless, there were encouraging signs of change in relation to employment and the involvement of ethnic minority communities.

Despite its small size, the ethnic minority communities are unevenly spread through the authority. Figures based on the school population show that although for the borough as a whole the proportion of children with parents from the New Commonwealth is 17 per cent, this varies from seven per cent to 30 per cent according to the district. The origins of the residents in North Thames are particularly varied as the area has received immigrants from many parts of the world at different times. Unlike South Thames, where the majority of the ethnic minority families originate from the Caribbean and have only lived in England for one or two generations, North Thames has many families who settled many decades ago and whose origins extend to Asia, Africa and the Mediterranean as well as the Caribbean.

South Thames
Both North Thames and South Thames are Inner London boroughs and they share certain similarities, both have long settled working class communities, areas of extreme affluence and poverty, and a rich ethnic mix. Yet alongside these similarities, differences can be pinpointed. Politically, South Thames is a Conservative borough; indeed, it is often referred to with as much pride by the right as North Thames is by the left. It is larger than North Thames and less densely populated, leafier, quieter and more suburban. South Thames is in some instances less deprived than either North Thames or Inner London as a whole. For example, figures for the academic year 1984/5 show that whereas 46 per cent of North Thames primary school children were eligible for free meals (and 44.5 per cent of children in ILEA all schools), the percentage for South Thames is 40.3 per cent. Similarly, for secondary school pupils, North Thames 44.8 per cent compares with the overall ILEA figure of 39.6 per cent while South Thames is only 35 percent.

As in North Thames, the Social Services Department in South Thames has a strong community orientation and the trend during the 1980s has been the development in patch work. This provides services within a small geographical area and draws on links with local people and their networks to inform the service and help define priorities. Unlike North Thames, where local offices provide a base for other departments as well as social services (housing and environmental health, for example), South Thames do not 'share' premises in this way. Nor is there any great emphasis on uniformity between area offices.

During the 1980s some re-organisation has taken place but at a speed to suit the areas, not according to a calendar of change imposed from above. Each area has handled its re-organisation separately and although some offices have favoured patch work, it has not been adopted throughout the department. The autonomy which is evident among the areas is also evident within them. Individual members of staff have been encouraged to develop their careers as senior practitioners if they wish to continue direct work with clients, and therefore do not have to ascend the managerial ladder in order to improve their pay and status. This, together with the fact that almost every member of the fieldwork staff is qualified, results in a powerful and vocal group of social workers in area offices. It means that initiatives often start in the field and are later accepted and facilitated by management rather than the other way round. An example of this has been the establishment of resource centres which are housed in buildings which were formerly short-stay children's homes. Their redesignation as resource centres has created establishments which can offer a residential base to whole families.

Resource centres are attached to areas but, like other aspects of the service provided by South Thames, they seek to respond to local need rather than achieve uniformity. The scope of their work is extensive with the only major constraints being space and time. Space limits the number of residents, but the ten beds at each centre can accommodate any permutation of family group, e.g. single parents and children, one large family or several small ones. Time is limited to a ten week period of residence which can be extended by negotiation. However, many people move out very quickly. Most, but not all, of the resident children are in care and most families are local. Again this can vary as some people will have very good reasons for living away from the neighbourhood in which they are known. Methods used for working with residents are wide ranging and include family therapy, groupwork and work programmes for individuals. Resource centres were still relatively new when our fieldwork was taking place and we were not in a position to evaluate their achievements. However, they were an impressive initiative and provided a type of service which was rare among our project authorities.

South Thames places very little value on documents to provide guidance on practice and procedure for social workers. This is in direct contrast to all our other authorities which seemed with varying degrees of intensity to be either writing weighty documents or blaming many of their problems on the fact that none existed. The attitude in South Thames is that a worker who is professionally qualified and experienced should not need to consult a manual in order to make a decision.

This approach provides a particularly stark contrast with District where levels of qualified staff are kept low on purpose and where management acknowledged that they recruit a number of newly qualified staff who will move to higher paying departments as soon as they have accrued some experience. No conclusions are drawn from this comparison. After all, a department may equally be censured for being full of 'dead wood' as for employing 'raw recruits'. But at times it really was difficult to believe that one was observing the same type of service in the same type of department at the same point in time.

3 Patterns of placement

Anyone interested in placement outcomes has to be concerned with placement inputs. Achievements only make sense in relation to aims. The length of a placement is much more relevant when set against its expected length. 'What happened next' needs to be seen in the context of the overall plan and questions inevitably arise about choice, emergencies and the legal route into care. Thus we knew from the beginning of the project that it would be important to gather information about placement starts as well as endings, but it was only when we struggled to understand our findings and make comparisons between authorities that we fully appreciated how crucial this would be.

When the project began, there was remarkably little information available about children in care apart from the DHSS annual return. This gives such basic facts as numbers, ages and legal status but can provide only a superficial and static picture. Between 1983 and 1986 a series of research reports provided an avalanche of new information. Packman and her colleagues[1] showed up major differences in the children being taken into care in two local authorities. They advanced our understanding of the different groups of children coming into care and helpfully categorised them as 'victims', 'villains' and 'volunteered'. Millham and his colleagues in the Dartington Social Research Unit followed a cohort of 450 children for two years and their report[2] provided a wealth of data on children's care experiences. More recently, from Fife and Leicestershire[3] comes information about children's length of stay in care, demonstrating a remarkable uniformity in the length of care episodes in two very different authorities. In Essex, Wedge and Phelan[4] have been monitoring child care services for the period 1981-5.

So, in presenting our findings on patterns of care we have concentrated on those aspects which serve to complement or challenge the facts and insights of previous studies. Our sample enables us to examine and highlight the rapid turnover of children in care and the number and type of placements which they experience. We are able to look at care experiences in relation to aim and plan as well as age and legal status. We can compare patterns in our six authorities with Packman's two authorities and consider which patterns seem to be more usual. We can do the same with care episodes, comparing our authorities with Leicestershire and Fife and with the Dartington cohort. And because we have some data on children whose placements are ending after many years, we can offer some information on long-stay cases which other cohort studies have not included.

The complexity of the project data base makes it necessary to keep defining the group under discussion. On many topics it is most satisfactory to confine the base to admissions or placements which occurred during the first year because this allows at least a 12-month period in which to follow developments. In order to avoid switching the data base, we quite often stick to Year 1 data in this report, even when both years could be included.

In this chapter (with the exception of the final section and a brief reference to place of safety orders made during Year 2), we are using three data bases:
1   The cohort of 2010 children who had one or more admissions in Year 1. (We can trace the re-admissions, moves and placements of this cohort of children over the two year period of the project.)
2   The 2353 admissions which the cohort children experienced during Year 1.
3   The 4940 placements which started in Year 1. (These include the 2353 admission placements and the subsequent moves of the cohort children. Also included are the move placements of children who were already in care when the project started.)

Admissions
Numbers, age and gender
The first point to note about admissions is how many of them there were. Heavy emphasis on the reduction in the number of children in care has tended to mask the reality that admissions have not declined nearly so much. The DHSS figures show that in the first half of the decade, the number of children in care declined by about 20,000 but the number of admissions only went down by about 10,000. There is evidently a more rapid turnover of care cases now and workloads will not have decreased in the way the statistics about children in care

might lead people to expect. Certainly the project authorities must have had a great deal of work dealing with nearly two and a half thousand admissions in a 12-month period.

The differences between end of year figures and figures demonstrating the turnover of children in care is highlighted by comparison of age groups at year end and at admission. DHSS annual returns show that as of 31 March in any year, only about one child in ten is a preschooler compared with more than one in four aged 16. The older age groups contain not only recent teenage admissions but young people admitted some years before and growing up in care.

This preponderance of adolescents creates the impression that the child care service is largely concerned with teenagers. Our findings (which are very similar to the most recent DHSS return), show that more than half of all admissions are children under 11 years old with more than a third being under five.

Table 3.1

Year 1 admissions by age and gender

	All	Male	Female
N =	2353	1343	1010
0–4	35%	34%	36%
5–10	21%	21%	20%
11–13	14%	15%	13%
14–15	22%	20%	24%
16+	8%	10%	6%

Note: In this and all subsequent tables, percentages are rounded and may not add to 100%.

The Dartington study drew attention to the relatively large number of infants under one year old being admitted to care. Their cohort included 11 per cent of infants. Our Year 1 admissions include 236 infants (12%), but it is noteworthy that half of them were specifically admitted for adoption. After the first year of life, the next most vulnerable years for admission to care are 14 and 15. Girls seem particularly prone to coming into care at this age. Indeed, nearly one in four of female admissions occurred in these two mid-teen years. After that, admissions of girls drop sharply. Boys have a rather more even spread of admissions across the years from 11-16 although their admissions also peak at 14-15.

Over all age groups, our Year 1 admissions divide into 43 per cent girls and 57 per cent boys. This is exactly the same as the DHSS return for the same year.

Figure 3.1 compares the age patterns at admission in the six project authorities. On the whole, these are similar but there are a few distinct differences. Since this is the first of what will be many occasions on which we compare the authorities in the light of our findings, it seems important to set the statistics in context and interpret them carefully.

Figure 3.1
Age at admission (Year 1 cohort)

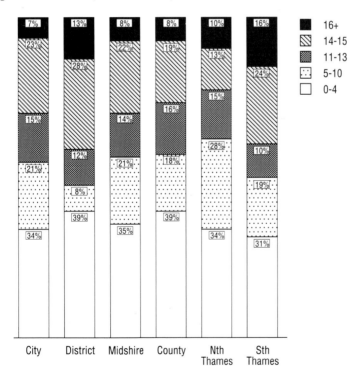

	16+
	14-15
	11-13
	5-10
	0-4

City   District   Midshire   County   Nth Thames   Sth Thames

The proportions of children of different ages which an authority admits will be affected by many factors including: the number of children of each age in the population; the authority's own policies and provision (for example, adoption programmes, Intermediate Treatment schemes or preventive services for young families); the policy and practice of other agencies (for example, courts and police).

We are not in a position to weigh the influence of these factors accurately but when we bring together our descriptive and statistical data, we see them at work. For example, District appears to admit rather few five to ten year olds, but we cannot conclude that children in this age group living in District are being denied help or are not needing child care services. It may be so, but it is more likely that this pattern is due both to District's active adoption programme (which increases admissions of infants) and to a large number of adolescent referrals from the courts. (District has the highest proportion of remands to care of all the project authorities.)

When compared with District, North Thames has a very large intake of five to tens (29 per cent against District's eight per cent), and far fewer teenage* admissions (35 per cent compared with 50 per cent in District). No doubt part of this five-to-ten 'bulge' in North Thames can be attributed to this authority's use of short stays in care as part of its support for families. But there are other possible explanations including demographic differences. Later in this chapter, we draw attention to what appear to be marked differences in the relationships between social services departments and the courts. In North Thames, comparatively few young people are admitted to care on remand (ten per cent of teenage admissions compared with 30 per cent in District).

Whereas North Thames has the lowest proportion of teenage admissions of the six authorities (34%), South Thames has one of the highest (51%). This is rather striking because, as in North Thames, the population of this London borough contains a smaller than average proportion of school-age children. However, once again the obvious explanation may not be entirely correct. The preponderance of adolescent admissions in South Thames may be due in large part to

---

* Throughout this report, we often use 'teenagers' and 'adolescents' as alternatives to tedious repetition of 'the 11+ age group'.

this authority's strong preventive services for young families. If few young children are admitted to care – and South Thames admits the lowest percentage of pre-schoolers – adolescents will make up a larger proportion of the total.

Re-admissions

Because of concern about re-admissions to care, the Dartington Research Unit conducted a small follow-up study of their cohort and found that of 280 children and adolescents who left care, 62 (22%) had a second admission and 17 (6%) had a third within two years. Our youngsters had similar experiences. Within the two years of our project, 18 per cent of those admitted during the first year had had a second admission and a further seven per cent had three or more. If we had been able to make follow-up enquiries in the third year, we would probably have learned of still more re-admissions, bringing our rate at least as high as the Dartington cohort and possibly higher. We would very much like to have investigated whether the 139 children who had three or more admissions went back to the same placements, but unfortunately time did not permit this. What we were able to establish was that re-admissions are not confined to young children. It is true that pre-schoolers accounted for six of the nine children who had five or more admissions, but nearly a quarter of the adolescents had at least one re-admission during the project.

This picture of frequent re-admissions is backed up by our finding that overall a third of the children in our Year 1 cohort had been in care on one or more previous occasions. This was true for only one in five of the pre-schoolers, but an astonishing 49 per cent of those aged five to ten had experienced at least one previous admission as had 38 per cent of the adolescents. The Dartington study, based on admissions in 1980, reports only 29 per cent of those admitted as having been in care before. Our somewhat higher figure may be due to different policies and practices in our sample authorities but one wonders whether the current emphasis on returning children home as swiftly as possible is inevitably swelling the re-admission rate in all social services departments.

At a conference in 1986, David Thorpe reported on his analysis of admissions, discharges and moves in Leicestershire. He found a substantial group of children who were regularly and frequently admitted to care for very brief periods returning always to the same accommodation. However, in our authorities, regular, planned respite care does not account for the re-admissions. We analysed the children in our Year 1 cohort who were admitted for temporary care (this heading included respite care). There were just six children with five or more temporary care admissions and four of them came from North Thames.

Emergency admissions
Both the Packman and Dartington studies commented on the high proportion of emergency admissions they encountered and linked these hasty placements with lack of preparation and planning. It is therefore rather depressing to have to report that no less than 74 per cent of our admissions are described by social workers as 'emergencies'. This is made up of 16 per cent new referrals and 58 per cent 'emergency though child/family already known to the department.' It seems that only one child in four experienced a planned, unrushed admission. In just one authority, County, this proportion rose to one in three.

Plan at admission
In the light of all the current emphasis on returning children to their own families, it was at first sight rather surprising to discover that at admission, the stated plan for less than half of them was 'return home'. Indeed, for adolescents, this figure dropped to 34 per cent. However, a closer look revealed that only 12 per cent of the whole group were definitely expected to stay in care, with a further five per cent destined for adoption. Next to 'return home', the largest group (24%) was made up of those for whom no plan had been made and this must surely be linked with the number of emergency admissions. Early adolescence shows up as a particularly difficult time to enter care as the 11-13 age group had the highest proportion expected to remain in care (21%) and the highest proportion where no plan was yet made (36%).

Within this overall pattern, there were very noticeable differences between authorities. City had the largest proportion of admissions with no plan yet made. County and District had the most adoption plans and South Thames topped the list for 'move to independence'. This is, of course, in line with the above average proportion of older teenagers being admitted to care in South Thames.

Legal status
The legal route by which a child enters care is important on several counts. It is likely to affect the way the child and family feel about the admission. It affects the departments' powers and, probably, social workers' attitudes to the case. Recent studies have also pointed to the association between legal status and length of stay in care.[2,3] Much has been written, too, about the increasing use of compulsory powers, so we thought we might find a majority of entrants to care coming by the compulsory route including place of safety orders. Based on the Dartington and Packman studies, we also expected to find considerable variation between our six authorities. In fact, for five out of the six authorities, two-thirds of admissions were voluntary and in North Thames this proportion rose to 77 per cent. City stands out as being rather different with only 55 per cent voluntary admissions and a distinct leaning toward compulsory measures. But even City looks much more like Packman's 'Clayport' than like 'Shiptown' where only a third of all admissions were voluntary. Overall 65 per cent of the Year 1 admissions were voluntary, but this did vary considerably according to age. While almost three out of four of the under 11s were admitted voluntarily under S.2 of the Children Act 1980 or the Adoption Act 1980, this declined to less than two out of three young teenagers, just over half of those in their middle teens and only two out of five of those aged 16. For this oldest group, remands made up 42 per cent of their admissions.

Chapter 10 will provide some detailed information about the 'offenders'* in our sample. For the moment, it must suffice to say that there were noteworthy differences in the proportion of admissions to our six authorities which had offender status. The range was from six per cent to 14 per cent of all Year 1 admissions and from 14 per cent to 30 per cent of admissions of adolescents. The role of social services departments in dealing with young offenders was beyond the scope of this project but, as we analysed our data, we could not help being aware

---

*'Offenders' in this study are defined by legal status, i.e. those on remand between court appearances, and on S.7.7 care orders after criminal proceedings. (This is, of course, a much smaller group than those who have committed offences.) We have also included those on care orders made in civil proceedings for non-attendance at school.

of its importance, not least in terms of workloads and use of resources.

Place of safety orders were of special interest to us because of concern over their increasing use and because the Jasmine Beckford enquiry's report was published about the middle of our project and we wondered whether the national emphasis on child abuse would be reflected in an increase of these orders. No very clear picture has emerged, but it does seem that the very high proportion of teenage place of safety orders reported by Packman in 'Shiptown' was atypical.

In our Year 1 sample, 17 per cent of all admissions were under place of safety orders which were used for 20 per cent of admissions of children aged under 11 and 13 per cent of the over 11s. (This percentage is very similar to DHSS figures but slightly lower than those reported in a study by the Dartington Research Team.)[5] Place of safety orders formed 22 per cent of City's Year 1 admissions but only 12 per cent of County's and seven per cent of South Thames'. However, these two latter authorities had rather more children admitted on care orders at admission (13 per cent and 16 per cent compared to City's seven per cent).

There was a slight increase in place of safety orders during the second year of the project, 429 compared to 402. We plotted the number of orders made in each quarter for the two year period. There was a slight upsurge after the Beckford Report but, curiously, in orders on adolescents not on younger children. The peak period for them was October-December 1986 but numbers dropped back again and in the final quarter of the project in early 1987 were virtually the same as when the project started in 1985 for both under 11s and teenagers.

The care experience
Type of placement
Patterns of placement vary considerably from one authority to another and also according to age. Although all authorities work under the same legislation, the children for whom they are responsible certainly do not have similar care experiences. Table 3.2 sets out the general pattern of each authority's placements in Year 1.

District and Midshire offer particularly striking differences in the way they provide for their children. It is not possible to show all the age groups in one table, but a primary school child in care in District is four

Table 3.2

Year 1 placements by type

	All	City	District	Mid-shire	County	North Thames	South Thames
N =	4940	1987	363	910	873	486	321*
Foster home	1837	37%	33%	26%	43%	42%	45%	34%
Adoption	102	2%	1%	3%	2%	4%	1%	1%
Residential	1859	37%	41%	51%	27%	33%	37%	40%
Lodgings	172	3%	2%	2%	7%	5%	1%	–
Home on trial	471	10%	10%	11%	11%	8%	5%	9%
Other inc. penal	499	11%	13%	7%	10%	8%	10%	15%

*In this and all subsequent tables, South Thames figures are for 6 months or 18 months as appropriate.

times as likely to have had a placement in a residential establishment as a child of the same age in care in Midshire. Even greater differences can be seen in home on trial placements for pre-schoolers – two per cent in District and 14 per cent in Midshire. The contrasts continue up the age scale with 26 per cent of teenage placements in District in an Observation and Assessment Centre compared with three per cent in Midshire. The use of lodgings is also very different in these authorities. In Midshire, (which appears to make unusually heavy use of this form of provision), lodgings provided 13 per cent of its Year 1 teenage placements compared with two per cent in District. Similar, though often less extreme, differences can be found when other authorities are compared.

The proportion of its annual placements which are in foster homes might appropriately be called an authority's foster-placement rate. It is interesting to compare the project authorities' Year 1 foster-placement rates with their boarding-out rates for the same year derived from the DHSS's annual return. The boarding out rate gives the percentage of children in care who are living in foster homes at one point in time, 31 March. It includes considerable numbers of children in long-stay foster placements who would not appear in the project's figures. The foster-placement rate reflects the turnover of children in foster homes during the year and is strongly affected by the amount of short-stay fostering work which an authority undertakes.

Table 3.3

DHSS Boarding-out rate 1985		Year 1 Foster placement rate	
Midshire	68%	N. Thames	45%
County	65%	Midshire	43%
District	57%	County	42%
S. Thames	50%	S. Thames	34%
City	48%	City	33%
N. Thames	48%	District	26%
Average for the six authorities	56%	Average for the six authorities	37%

The differences between boarding-out rates and foster-placement rates are sometimes quite dramatic. Thus North Thames, which ties with City for the lowest boarding-out rate among the six authorities, can be shown to have the highest foster-placement rate. By contrast, District, with a fairly high boarding-out rate sinks to the bottom of the foster-placement rate. This reversal comes about because North Thames does a great deal of very short-term fostering, while District evidently has a substantial number of settled, long-term foster children who did not appear in the project sample but swell the boarding-out figures.

It seems clear that the static picture provided by the boarding-out rate can be misleading. It has over-emphasised the part foster care plays in providing placements and it is not a very satisfactory basis for making comparisons between authorities, especially if a high boarding-out rate is considered meritorious. Well-developed preventive services, the use of residential family centres and emphasis on task focussed and time-limited foster placements instead of long-term fostering can all have the effect of lowering the boarding-out rate. The decline in long-term fostering means that as teenagers who are currently in long-term foster homes graduate out of the system, authorities are likely to find that their DHSS boarding-out rates dip noticeably, even if they are making a higher proportion of placements in foster homes than ever before.

The pie charts in Figure 3.2 provide a quick way to compare the pattern of placements for different age groups. They make clear the continued importance of the residential sector for older children. Our findings on the continued importance of the residential sector re-affirm those of Millham and Berridge.[6] Most pre-school placements are in foster or adoptive homes, but residential establishments of various types still deal with more than half of all placements of adolescents (52 per cent in Year 1). For adolescents, the range of

Figure 3.2
Type of placement, by age

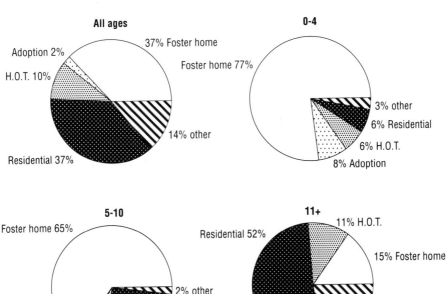

possible placement is increased by the use of lodgings, hostels and bed-sits or own flats and penal establishments but the small proportion of teenage foster placements, only 15 per cent, is striking.

Suitability of placement
In spite of the considerable variation in the type of placements used, there were only rather small differences between the authorities in the proportion of placements which social workers considered 'doubtful' or 'unsuitable'. In the two counties and the two London boroughs getting on for one placement in five (17%-18%) fell into these categories. City and District's social workers were somewhat more sanguine about the suitability of the placements they used and their rates for 'doubtful' or 'unsuitable' placements were 13 per cent and 15 per cent respectively. It is worth noting that social workers in City and District were also the most likely to feel that they had had choice about their placements. In 44 per cent of City placements and 47 per cent of District's, social workers reported that they had at least some choice. This was true of only 33 per cent of Midshire's placements, 34 per cent in South Thames, 35 per cent in County and 39 per cent in North Thames.

Placement aims
We deliberately did not ask about reasons for admission because we needed to use the same questionnaires for all placements, whether these were happening at admission or years later. However, we did ask social workers to select an aim for each placement. Once again there are considerable differences between authorities due in part to the type of child being admitted and in part to policy and practice. Thus for admission placements, County clearly puts considerable emphasis on assessment, while Midshire stresses treatment. North Thames is much the most likely to use temporary care for both young children and adolescents and in City the provision of 'emergency roof over head' looms large, fitting with City's high rate of emergency, unplanned admissions.

The aims of admission placements are, of course, often different from those of subsequent placements. It is interesting to contrast aims at admission with aims of placements which follow a move in care. (These include placements home on trial.) Such a comparison shows that there are rather few admission placements which have the aim of care and upbringing but this is the aim for about one placement in five following a move. The provision of temporary care is the purpose of nearly a third of admission placements but, since most of these children go straight home again, few subsequent placements have this aim. Just as one would expect, move placements are much more likely than are admission placements to have 'bridge to independence' as their aim. Less expected is the finding that one move placement in ten is given the aim 'emergency/roof over head'. This has to be seen as a salutary reminder of the instability of the care experience.

Numbers of moves and placements
Since researchers use different methods for calculating the number of moves a child may have, it is necessary to be cautious and read the fine print before making any comparisons. We decided not to count admissions and discharges as moves but to limit ourselves to moves within the care system. (Return home on trial counts as a move because the child is still in care.) Readers will recall that when defining a 'placement' we decided to exclude holidays and trial visits and not to attempt to include all changes of residence of young people living independently. Our 'moves' are also minimum figures because we cannot know how many more moves will be experienced by the children who were still in care at the end of the project. Our figures are based on the cumulative number of moves experienced during the project by the cohort of 2010 children with at least one admission in Year 1. (Since the fieldwork lasted two years, the maximum period in which moves might occur was 23 months and the minimum 12 months.)

It is encouraging to report that more than half the cohort children (57%) had no moves. However, 26 per cent had one move, nine per cent had two, and eight per cent had three or more. There were 38 unfortunate youngsters who had five or more moves in this relatively short time and, sadly, six of them were pre-schoolers. It is the 16-17 year olds who move most: 15 per cent of them had three or more moves during the project. The 14-15 year olds had almost as many. The five to tens move least but, as we shall see below, they are the most prone to drift on in placements. There are no startling differences between authorities though the proportion of children having three or more moves varies from six per cent (City and District) to 11 per cent (Midshire).

Children may undergo change as a result of discharge and re-admission as well as having moves within the care system. So in some ways, the best indicator of their experience is to count the number of placements they have had. Two children may each have had four placements, one of them as a result of four separate admissions while the other may have had only one admission followed by three moves. Less than half of our cohort (44%) had only one placement during the project and 28 per cent had three or more placements. Apart from those young people who were 16 on admission to care, the five to tens were the most stable; 51 per cent had only one placement and another 26 per cent had only two. The under-fives did not fare quite so well and 25 per cent of them experienced three or more placements – in fact 33 (5%) had five or more.

Overall, 32 per cent of adolescents had at least three placements but when this is broken down into 'offenders' and 'non-offenders' and by age band, interesting differences emerge. Of the 'non-offending' 11-13 year olds, 22 per cent had at least three placements, but this is no more than the five to tens group. In strong contrast, their contemporaries who came into care as offenders have the most placements of any age group (57 per cent with at least three). The 14-15 year old offenders are close runners up with 55 per cent having had at least three placements. This compares with 30 per cent non-offending 14-15 year olds with three or more placements which is the same picture as non-offending 16s and 17s, 30 per cent of whom also had three or more moves. Offenders aged 16 have rather few placements because they tend to stay longer in penal establishments.

We were not in a position to evaluate the benefits or damage moves might bring but as we processed questionnaires and kept track of the children's experiences we could not help being aware of various patterns and realised how potentially misleading a straight counting of moves might be. For instance, how can one compare the move to a foster family for a child who has spent three nights in a children's home after being admitted in an emergency, with a move into a residential establishment after a long-term foster home breakdown? A series of moves between penal establishments coming in quick succession must have a very different impact from moves between foster homes or children's homes which come several months apart and involve changing schools and local friends, yet all must count alike in a statistical survey such as this one.

It seemed to us that there were patterns of moves that were unpredictable but clearly recognisable in retrospect. We frequently plotted a string of moves for an adolescent who was 'on a tear' and uncontainable for a while. Then suddenly a placement would 'fit' and we would hear no more of him or her. Sometimes it seemed to go the other way and, usually following the breakdown of a stable placement, a youngster seemed to go into a downward spiral with a series of increasingly unsatisfactory placements ending perhaps in secure accommodation or a penal establishment.

Expected length of placement
There were few surprises in our data on expected length of placement except for the remarkable uniformity we found across the six authorities. Although, as we have seen, they take in somewhat different groups of children and make markedly different use of residential care, there are few differences in social workers' expectations of placement length. North Thames is the one exception. Linked with its frequent use of temporary care, more North Thames placements are expected to be very short (38 per cent less than a month compared with the average of 27 per cent). Correspondingly few North Thames placements are intended to be really long term (six per cent for five or more years or 'permanently'.) The other London borough is the same in this respect but in the remaining four authorities ten to 11 per cent of their placements are planned to last five years or more.

The overall pattern is for young children to have placements expected to last either less than six months or permanently, while teenagers' placements show a more even spread across the time bands with about one placement in five expected to be of intermediate length, i.e. more than six months but less than five years. The most usual expected placement length for teenagers is two to six months whereas for under 11s it is one to three weeks. How these expectations compared with reality will be explored in the following chapter.

Care episodes
The length of time children and young people spend in care has been a matter of concern ever since the publication of *Children who wait* in 1973.[7] A series of recent studies from the Dartington Research Unit,[2] The National Children's Bureau,[8] Leicestershire and Fife[3] have now explored the different rates of discharge for various groups of children. They have produced a 'leaving care curve' which graphically portrays

the rates at which children leave care. About half go out of care within a few weeks but after that the flow of discharges diminishes to a trickle and a substantial minority remain in care indefinitely. A third of the Leicestershire and Fife children were still in care after a year and 38 per cent of the Dartington cohort remained in care after two years.

Our sample is not absolutely comparable with either of these studies in the time period covered. If we take our Year 1 admissions, we can report on their situation at the end of the second year when at least 12 months would have elapsed since they entered care. Our discharges fall along a curve very similar to the other studies – with a steep rise in the early weeks followed by a sudden flattening out.

Figure 3.3
Leaving care curve

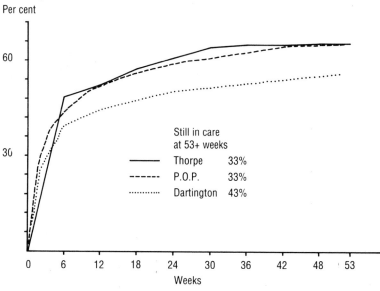

Thirty-five per cent of the project children had left care within the first month, a further 11 per cent went in the next four weeks and 15 per cent between two and six months. Only six per cent left between the sixth and twelfth month and a mere two per cent in the whole of the second year. Thus we can fully confirm the previous findings that if

50

children do not leave care quickly they may well remain a very long time.

However, though our discharge pattern is so similar, the overall findings of these studies are by no means identical. Our discharge rate is much more like Leicestershire and Fife than like the Dartington cohort. Only 31 per cent of our Year 1 children were still in care when the project ended. Thirty-three per cent of the Leicester and Fife youngsters were still in care after a year, but 38 per cent of the Dartington cohort remained after two years.

Both Thorpe and Millham stress that their 'stayers' were predominantly adolescents. In the Dartington cohort only 21 per cent of the under-fives were still in care two years after admission compared with 51 per cent of their teenagers. In Leicester the pattern was the same and a much higher proportion of teenagers remained in care for more than 12 months. We, too, found that adolescents are more prone to remain in care than are younger children but the difference was much less extreme. Taking our Year 1 admissions, 28 per cent of under 5s were still in care at project end, 30 per cent of five to tens, 39 per cent of 11-13s and 36 per cent of 14-15s. As one would expect, few of those aged 16 at admission stay long in care and only 19 per cent remained by the end of our second year.

This pattern of fewer young children and more adolescents remaining holds good for all our six authorities but there are considerable differences in their overall percentages of 'stayers'. The range is from 21 per cent in District to 43 per cent in County. Chapter 2 has drawn attention to County's special schemes for providing 'time out' relief breaks for families without admission to care. These must forestall many very short-term admissions, but it is still difficult to explain County's very high proportion of 'stayers' especially as they admit more young children than any other authority. However, it does fit with their higher than average figures for children where 'remain in care' is the plan at admission and the Dartington researchers have stressed the importance of social workers' expectations in determining children's length of stay.

Both Millham and Thorpe have stressed the strong association between the legal route of entry to care and length of stay. Our data entirely support this view. Only 22 per cent of project children who were admitted voluntarily were still in care a year or more later compared with 47 per cent of those admitted compulsorily. We had somewhat fewer place of safety orders than the Dartington study but the 17 per cent of children who were admitted on these orders formed 29 per cent of our 'stayers'. Only ten per cent of project children were admitted on a court order (excluding remands) but they formed 21 per cent of 'stayers'.

The Dartington research team and Packman have all highlighted the feelings of anger and outrage raised in some parents whose children are compulsorily removed and no doubt young people on court orders often feel equally angry and unco-operative. It seems inherently probable that the method of entry to care affects both duration and outcome. Nevertheless, it seems too simplistic to imply that legal status of itself causes prolonged stays and unfortunately a survey such as ours could not even begin to tease out the subtle interaction of family and child problems and attitudes, social work and court interventions and the cumulative effect of the care system on all those involved. All we can do is to re-affirm the links between legal status and length of stay which appeared strongly in all our authorities.

The stayers
Of course we do not know what will happen to those children and young people who remained in care when the project ended, but we can get some ideas from outcomes of long-term placements which ended during the project. Information about these will be given in the subsequent chapters of this book. We also have some data on the large group of 923 children in our sample who were already in care when the project began, were still in care when it ended and had no discharges or re-admissions in between. This group really does deserve the name 'stayers' for it contains the long-term but unsettled children of the care system.

These 923 'stayers' were predominantly teenagers (78 per cent were aged 11). They were spread across the six authorities in very much the same proportions as other children in the project sample. They all came into the project on a move and exactly two thirds of them had been in the placement they were leaving for more than a year. About one in four had been there for three or more years.

These moves included young people going into more independent accommodation and children and teenagers going home on trial as well as more problematic moves. Thirty-four youngsters were leaving residential establishments in which they had lived for more than a year because the establishment was closing and 56 had to leave foster homes where they had been for more than a year because of some unexpected and disruptive event in the foster family. Overall, the behaviour of more than one in four (27%) was said to have been unacceptable to care givers.

Only 17 per cent of the stayers were still in voluntary care. Eighteen per cent were now under S.3 of the Children Act 1980 but the largest group (56%) were under a care order. Most of the remaining nine per cent were wards of court or placed in care under matrimonial or guardianship acts.

By the end of the project, more than two thirds were in what was intended to be a final or permanent placement. For just 35 of them (4%) the last placement's aim was adoption. For 332 (36%) the aim was care and upbringing while for almost as many (30%) the placement was seen as a bridge to independence. Among the remaining 30 per cent were 43 unfortunate youngsters still considered to be in need of assessment and a similar number whose last project placement was aiming only at emergency/roof over head.

Except for the 182 children (20%) whose last placement was home on trial, very few were expected to return home. Nearly a third were in foster or adoptive homes (31%), slightly fewer (27%) were in residential establishments. Lodgings (6%), flats or bed-sits (7%) and hostels (4%) were providing a bridge to independent life out of care for some and, as mentioned above, 20 per cent were at home on trial. This leaves five per cent in a variety of placements from boarding school to penal establishment.

Thus for most of the stayers some kind of stability had been achieved at least in intention. However, we know that one unsuccessful placement is apt to lead to another and many of these youngsters had had very unsettled careers in care. Half of them had more than one move during the two years of the project and 29 per cent had at least three moves in this period. There were 80 (of whom half were young people aged 14 or 15) who had at least five moves during the project and we have to bear in mind that many stayers will have had several placement changes before the project started. With this history, it seems only too likely that for many, further changes will occur.

References

1 Packman J with Randall J and Jacques N *Who needs care* Blackwell, 1986.

2 Millham S, Bullock R, Hosie K and Haak M *Lost in care* Gower, 1986.

3 Thorpe D 'Career patterns in child care – implications for the service' *British Journal of Social Work* 18 2, 1987.

4 Wedge P and Phelan J 'Reports on child care in Essex' *Social Work Today* 19: 35, 39 and 41, 1988.

5 Millham S et al *Place of Safety Orders Report to the DHSS*, 1984.

6 Berridge D *Children's homes* Blackwell, 1985.

7 Rowe J and Lambert L *Children who wait* ABAFA, 1973.

8 Vernon J and Fruin D *In care. A study of social work decision making* National Children's Bureau, 1986.

4 Patterns of outcome

Study of the placements of children in care leaves an indelible impression of the immense amount of work involved. Admitting, moving and discharging children are time consuming and therefore expensive procedures so from a managerial as well as the even more important humanitarian point of view, it is essential to know as much as possible about how all these various placements turn out. Do they achieve their aims? Are they helpful to the children and young people who experience them? How long do they last and is this as long or longer than planned? What happens next? Do outcomes differ according to authority? Each question seems to give rise to another one.

We have found some answers to these questions, but they are seldom simple or even straightforward. Even as we try to set them out as clearly and accurately as possible, we are aware of the risk that they could be misleading. There are dangers in generalising from such a diverse range of ages and types of placement, though sometimes this needs to be done in order to present the total picture. There is also a danger of trying to evaluate outcomes when the study was mainly set up to monitor and lacks the depth needed for really adequate evaluation.

In Chapter 1 we drew attention to the potential risk of making spurious comparisons between authorities. There is also a risk of making inappropriate comparisons with other research findings. In another context,[1] we tried to highlight problems which can occur if foster breakdown rates are compared without careful study of the definitions of breakdown and of the type of foster placement being considered. A good example of this risk is presented in an as yet unpublished study of 'temporary' foster placements which was being undertaken in Strathclyde at the same time as our own survey. In the Strathclyde study, placements of less than four weeks were excluded and 'temporary' was defined as all other placements which were not intended to be permanent. Serious confusion would arise if the outcomes of these 'temporary' placements were to be compared with outcomes of foster placements in our study which had the aim 'temporary care', not least because most of our 'temporary care' foster placements were completed in less than four weeks and so would be excluded from the Strathclyde study.

But with these caveats in mind, we can present some answers to the questions posed earlier and offer a broad-sweep picture of the outcomes of the 9335 placements which ended during our survey. Subsequent chapters will examine different types of placement in greater detail and will look into differences between ethnic groups.

For most of this chapter, the data base is 'all placement endings'. When it is necessary to bring together the beginning and end of placements (as when looking at expected length and actual length), then the appropriate base is the 4163 Year 1 placements which ended during the project. If we are using Year 1 only, this is always mentioned.

How long did the placements last?

Whether by design or default, most child care placements of all types are rather short. We found that overall 71 per cent had ended within six months, and about one in three lasted less than four weeks. A mere six per cent of the completed placements which we studied had continued for more than three years, although 12 per cent of the placements which started during the project were intended to last at least that long.

If we take six months as a pivot point, there is little difference in the length of foster or residential placements, 71 per cent per cent of residential placements had ended by six months as had 75 per cent of foster placements. However, proportionately more foster than residential placements are very short – 47 per cent of foster placements lasted three weeks or less, compared with 31 per cent of residential – and more are very long – eight per cent of foster placements compared with four per cent of residential had lasted three or more years.

The questionnaires asked social workers to code whether placements had lasted as long as planned and also whether they had lasted as long as the children needed them. When all ages and types of placement are taken together, just half (51%) were said to have lasted as planned, a third (32%) not as long as planned and one in six (17%) had lasted longer. Age is clearly an important factor as Table 4.1 demonstrates. Placements of adolescents were twice as likely as those of pre-schoolers to end sooner than planned (38 per cent compared with 19 per cent) and the five to tens fell between with 25 per cent of early endings.

Table 4.1

Whether placement lasted as planned, by age

		All	0–4	5–10	11+
	N =	9335	2074	1325	5936
Lasted as planned		42%	56%	48%	36%
		(51%)	(63%)	(56%)	(45%)
Did not last as long as planned		26%	17%	21%	31%
		(32%)	(19%)	(25%)	(38%)
Lasted longer		15%	16%	17%	13%
		(17%)	(18%)	(19%)	(17%)
Not applicable (no plan re length)		16%	10%	14%	18%
NK		1%	1%	1%	2%

Note: The percentages in brackets exclude the 'not applicable/no plan' cases. This makes it possible to compare this table with Table 4.2 below.

Early endings can, of course, occur for excellent reasons. Family problems may be resolved more speedily than anticipated, or other, more suitable placements may become available sooner than expected. Similarly, extended stays sometimes occur just because a placement is being particularly beneficial. On the other hand, placement plans can go awry because of unexpected delays either waiting for court hearings or because resources such as adoptive or long-term foster families are not available. Lasting too long is not as frequent a problem as premature endings but affects a substantial number of children. Readers do need to bear in mind the differences in interpretation of 'lasted too long' which are discussed in the first chapter. 'Lasted too long' does not necessarily imply that the placement itself was unsatisfactory.

So far, we have been considering placement length in relation to social workers' plans. In order to meet changing circumstances, plans may often have to be revised. There is an important difference between this and whether or not the placement length matched the child's needs. It may happen that a placement ends sooner than originally planned but it has nevertheless lasted as long as needed. Conversely, a placement may last as planned but this turns out to be not long enough to meet the child's needs. Table 4.2 shows how the proportions of placements which did or did not last as long as needed varied according to the child's age.

Table 4.2

Whether placement lasted as needed, by age

		All	0–4	5–10	11+
	N =	9335	2074	1325	5936
Lasted as needed		62%	75%	67%	56%
Did not last as needed		22%	13%	18%	26%
Lasted too long		14%	9%	13%	16%
NK		2%	–	1%	2%

When Table 4.1 is compared with Table 4.2, the patterns are very similar. The percentage of placements that last as long as planned or needed declines steadily according to age. However, it is noticeable, though not surprising, that whereas there is virtually no difference between the age groups in the proportion of placements that lasted longer than planned, there is an age difference in the proportions said to have lasted longer than needed. Only nine per cent of the endings of the under-fives had lasted too long compared with 16 per cent of the 11 + age group. It is also worth pointing out that in every age group, the proportion of placements that did not last as long as needed is somewhat smaller than the proportion that did not last as long as planned. This results in a slightly more encouraging picture, but it must be a matter for concern, that one in every four placements of adolescents fails to last as long as needed.

The type of placement which most often failed to last as long as needed was home on trial. Across all age groups about one home on trial placement in three ended prematurely. There were much greater age differences in foster home endings as we shall see in Chapter 6. Residential placements were somewhat more likely than foster homes to last as long as necessary but comparisons are complicated by the need to take account of age and intended placement length.

Managers and those responsible for allocating resources may be interested to know more about the accuracy of social workers' predictions on placement length. Overall, 57 per cent lasted for the period expected, 19 per cent went on longer and 24 per cent ended sooner.

These averages conceal wide differences between the various time periods and some smaller differences between age groups. As one might expect, it was clearly easier for social workers to make correct estimates when placements were expected to be very short and much more difficult when the expected length was more than four weeks. Expectations of stays of less than four weeks turned out to be correct in nearly three cases out of four. By contrast, the average for the rest was just over one in three correct. Stays for the younger children were slightly more often correctly predicted than stays for adolescents. We also found that placements of younger children were somewhat more inclined to go on longer than expected while those of the teenagers tended to end sooner.

Placement drift

Placements that continue very much longer than expected are one aspect of the problem of drift in care. They have usually attracted much less attention than premature endings, so we wanted to learn what we could from our data.

The first finding is that encouragingly few of the new placements seemed subject to really serious drift. Out of nearly 5000 placements made by our six authorities in the first year of the project, only 110 (2%) were seriously overdue at project end.

It seems clear that drift in placement (which of course is not the same thing as drift in care), is a very small problem in comparison with premature endings and constant moves. Of these 110 'drifters', 54 were in foster homes, 48 in residential establishments, five home on trial and three in some other type of accommodation. Almost all the pre-schoolers in this group were in foster homes, as were two out of three of those aged five to ten. However, fewer than one in four of the teenagers drifting in placement were in foster homes.

When the percentage of 'drifters' in each authority is considered, we find that County had the highest proportion. (We saw in the previous chapter that County also had the highest percentage of children still in care after 12 months so this finding is not unexpected.) Young teenagers in residential care seemed particularly at risk of placement drift in County, but overall, it was the five to tens whose placements were most inclined to be unexpectedly prolonged. Five per cent of all Year 1 placements in this age band were affected in this way and it is worth noting that the Dartington researchers expressed particular concern about this age group.

What happened next?
Nearly half of all placements ended with the child moving on to another care facility and approximately half of the endings were discharges. We say 'approximately' because in a few instances a move to a flat coincided with an eighteenth birthday and a discharge from care and some moves to penal establishments were also discharges.

Within the discharge group, the vast majority went home. Only three per cent of our discharges followed an adoption order and two per cent occurred when care orders were revoked on children already living at home on trial. There were 633 young people (seven per cent of placement endings) who were leaving care at 18. About a third of them (30%) were living in foster families and another third (31%) were in lodgings or bed-sits or established in their own flat. A few were in custody, and 14 per cent were living at home on trial. There were just 124 youngsters who were being discharged from residential establishments and probably facing the uncertain future described by Stein and Carey.[2]

Numerically, the most common move was a transfer from one residential establishment to another. During the two years of the project there were 1098 such moves and they comprised 29 per cent of all residential endings. Moves between foster homes were also numerous and one in four foster placements ended with a move to another foster home. However, in percentage terms, the most frequent move was from one lodging to another. Lodgings were the least stable of all placements and 34 per cent ended with a move to other lodgings or a bed-sit.

Family contact

Because of the public and professional concern over access to children in care and the maintenance of family links, we wanted to learn all we could on this topic even though we recognised that our survey could produce only limited and superficial information. On the face of it, our findings provide a rather more encouraging picture than that presented in Millham and colleagues' report *Lost in care*.[3] Exact comparisons between the two studies are impossible but we wonder how much of the apparent improvement may be due to methodology. We had to rely entirely on pre-coded answers to a questionnaire while Millham had repeated interviews with social workers and also talked with some parents and young people.

In 29 per cent of the placements which ended during our project, the child had been placed with at least one sibling. The age group most likely to be placed with a sibling was the five to tens (65%). In only 15 per cent of placements which ended when the child concerned was aged 11 had a sibling been present but the equivalent figure for the under-fives was 44 per cent.

If the endings of home on trial placements are excluded, about three children out of every five had been having contact with their families at least once a month. (For 44 per cent contact was at least weekly.) One child in five had had no contact during the past six months but, as we shall see later, many placements were extremely brief and lack of contact in such circumstances may be unavoidable. It is noteworthy that in only two per cent of endings did social workers say that visits had not been allowed but there may, nevertheless, have been restrictions on the amount of contact.

Visits to young children seem more likely to be prohibited than visits to older ones, but if children placed for adoption are excluded, this difference largely disappears. Nor were overall differences in visiting patterns in foster homes or residential establishments as great as we had anticipated. We found that 44 per cent of children leaving foster homes had been seeing their family at least weekly as had 51 per cent of those leaving residential care.

Neither our data nor our resources allowed for complex analysis of visiting patterns controlling for factors like age, length of placement and type of placement. But we do have further clear evidence of the difficulty of maintaining family links for children in long-stay foster homes. At the end of the 269 foster home placements with non-relatives which had lasted at least three years, only 18 per cent of the children were said to have been having contact with their family as often as once a month and 38 per cent had had no contact at all during the previous six months. Most of the rest had had occasional contact but in five per cent the question was said to be 'not applicable' because no contact was possible.

Were the placements helpful?

There are considerable grounds for encouragement in the answers to this question though we need to remember that we are dealing with soft data and only have the social workers' perceptions of what the placement has achieved. Cynics may say that their judgements were over-optimistic but it could be a sign of thoughtful and discriminating judgement when a social worker codes a placement as not having lasted as long as intended, yet as having been helpful in spite of this.

Across the board, a third of all placement endings were rated as having been considered 'very helpful' and another 37 per cent 'fairly helpful' making a total of 71 per cent rated positively helpful. In ten per cent of cases social workers felt they could not make a judgement or there was no information so this leaves just 13 per cent of placements rated as 'not very helpful' and six per cent 'unhelpful'. Even for adolescents, only 22 per cent were rated as not helpful and there were remarkably positive ratings for teenage foster placements in spite of their proneness to premature endings (70 per cent very or fairly helpful). This interesting finding will be discussed more fully in the chapter on foster care.

As one might expect, social workers seldom considered penal placements to have been at all helpful. More surprising, 27 per cent of lodgings and 26 per cent of home on trial placements were thought to have been less than helpful.

There were noticeable differences between the authorities in the proportion of placements which social workers coded as having been either very or fairly helpful. County's social workers gave the most optimistic ratings and coded 78 per cent as at least fairly helpful. Much more pessimistic codings were made by social workers in City and South Thames. Although these two authorities differed from each other in so many respects, 66 per cent of placements in both were coded as very or fairly helpful.

How well did the placements meet their aims?
This is obviously a key question but one which it is very difficult to answer accurately and succinctly. The child care world has not been accustomed to classifying placements by aim and the emphasis has been more on the type of placement – for example, foster home or residential – or its expected length. But as we worked on the data emerging from this project, it became ever more evident that the aims of placements are a crucial factor in accounting for their outcomes. Common sense would suggest that some aims are much easier to achieve than others and our data certainly bear this out.

'Temporary care', 'treatment' and 'assessment' provide examples of three aims which present caregivers with a variety of tasks and have very different outcomes. Providing temporary care for a child or teenager who may be unhappy and disturbed will often be stressful and hard work. But the aim – to provide food, shelter and 'care' – is relatively easy to achieve in comparison with the aims of assessment or treatment which require the same care-giving plus specific, highly skilled work. So it is not surprising to find that the aims of assessment and treatment were seldom fully achieved.

Table 4.3

Extent aim achieved

Primary aim		Fully	In most respects	Only partially	Not at all	No info.
Temporary care	N = 1753					
	100%	63%	23%	11%	2%	1%
Assessment	N = 892					
	100%	20%	42%	29%	7%	1%
Treatment	N = 1060					
	100%	12%	30%	43%	13%	1%

As Table 4.3 shows, the aim of assessment was achieved in at least most respects in a substantial proportion of cases. But treatment is clearly very difficult and well over half of the treatment placements achieved their aim only partially or not at all. The contrast with temporary care could scarcely be more striking since 86 per cent of temporary care placements achieved this at least in most respects.

The child's age affects aims and outcomes in two ways. First, some aims apply mainly to older children (for example, 'bridge to independence'), or to the youngest ones (for example, 'adoption'). Except for the tiny group that fail completely, adoption aims were almost always reported as being fully met. 'Bridge to independence' is much harder to achieve and about half these placements succeeded 'only partially' or 'not at all' in meeting this aim.

Secondly, age has some effect on the extent to which aims of 'temporary care', 'assessment' and 'treatment' are achieved, with teenagers scoring somewhat lower in all categories, but the patterns hold good for all of them. It is also interesting to note that the type of placement often appears to make remarkably little difference. For example, figures based on placements made in the first year of the project show that temporary care for adolescents was achieved at least in most respects in 77 per cent of residential placement endings and in exactly the same proportion of foster placements. The much more difficult aim of 'treatment' had been achieved for 48 per cent of adolescents leaving residential establishments and for 51 per cent of those leaving foster homes.

Looking across all the 9335 placement endings the general picture is that in approximately a third the aim had been 'fully' met (36%), in another third it was met 'in most respects' (30%). In about one in five it was met 'only partially' (22%) and ten per cent of aims were considered not to have been met at all.

'Successful' and 'unsuccessful' outcomes
Our failure during the pilot work to find any satisfactory single measure of outcome was mentioned in the first chapter. We had to accept the impossibility of finding a method which would appropriately combine several different aspects of outcome and we became cautious about relying too much on social worker perceptions. Nevertheless, as we tried to get maximum benefit from our findings, we continually felt the need to have some simple classification which would make comparisons easier and might give social workers and managers some sense of what proportion of their placements 'turn out all right'.

We experimented with various ways of combining our outcomes data and finally decided that the simplest was the best. If a placement lasted as long as the child needed it and met the stated aim at least in most respects, it could be called 'successful'. If it did not last as long as the child needed it and the aim was met only partially or not at all, it should be considered 'unsuccessful'. This leaves unclassified those placements which have a mixed outcome, those, for example, which lasted but whose aims were not met or did not last quite as long as needed but whose aims were achieved in most respects. It ignores the question about helpfulness, does not take account of what happened next and makes no attempt to judge the quality of the placement. However, it does offer an opportunity to make some comparisons across authorities and between different types of placement. 'Success', on this basis, will, of course, be strongly affected by the ease or difficulty of the placement's aim, but since the aim is the whole purpose of the placement, this emphasis seems quite valid.

Using this crude measurement, we find that half of all placements which ended during the project were 'successful' and only 16 per cent were 'unsuccessful'. Age reduces the success rate from 70 per cent of under-fives, to 43 per cent of those who were over 11 when the placement ended. Conversely, the 'unsuccessful' rate doubles from nine per cent for under-fives to 20 per cent for adolescents. Many factors have to be considered when interpreting these findings and they will be discussed in subsequent chapters. For the three most usual types of placement the outcomes are set out in Table 4.4.

Table 4.4

'Successful' and 'unsuccessful' outcomes by types of placement

	Foster home	Residential establishment	Home on trial
N =	3554	3979	785
'Successful'	60%	46%	36%
'Unsuccessful'	15%	16%	27%
Mixed ratings	25%	38%	37%

Home on trial is clearly the least 'successful' type of placement, but comparisons must be somewhat suspect because it may well be that in these placements the risk of failure was known to be high. The fact that children in residential placements tend to be older than those going into foster homes also needs to be borne in mind when comparing 'success' rates. Subsequent chapters will show that for placements which ended in the teen years, the difference in 'success' rates of foster home and residential placements disappears. However, home on trial has the lowest 'success' rates for all age bands.

Do outcomes differ according to authority?

It may come as a surprise to readers to discover just how little difference there appears to be in the overall outcomes of the authorities' placements. Although we now realise that simple comparison of overall outcomes can be misleading, the degree of similarity, as shown in Table 4.5, still seems remarkable.

Table 4.5

'Successful' and 'unsuccessful' outcomes by authority

	All	City	District	Mid-shire	County	North Thames	South Thames
N =	9335	3311	640	1818	1623	1041	902
'Successful'	51%	51%	54%	54%	51%	50%	49%
'Unsuccessful'	16%	17%	14%	16%	16%	18%	15%
Mixed ratings	33%	32%	32%	30%	33%	32%	36%

However, these very similar overall outcomes conceal a number of differences in the authorities' 'success' rates for the various types of placement. Some of these differences occur when the total numbers are relatively small and/or unevenly spread and it would clearly be unwise to build too much on them. But the 'success' rate for foster care ranges from 56 per cent (South Thames) to 68 per cent (District), a statistically significant difference. For residential care, the range is too narrow to be significant but differences in the 'success' of home on trial placements are significant with a range from 27 per cent (District) to 48 per cent (Midshire).

These results need to be interpreted with caution. For instance, the differences between District and South Thames in successful fostering outcomes do not take account of important differences in the groups of children whose placements are being compared. When it comes to home on trial, we find that a third of Midshire's placements are pre-schoolers compared with only nine per cent in District.

When considering the remarkable similarity of residential outcomes, it is necessary to remember that the project's measure of 'success' says nothing about the quality of the service provided. To use a medical simile, it is rather like quoting a percentage of successful operations without any measure of the patients' hospital experiences in terms of waiting time for operations, facilities, food or nursing care. Had we been able to consult them, no doubt the consumers of the child care service would have reported just as varied an experience as do patients in hospital.

References

1 Rowe J 'Interpreting breakdown rates' *Adoption & Fostering* 11 1, 1987.

2 Stein M and Carey K *Leaving care* Blackwell 1986.

3 Millham S, Bullock R, Hosie K and Haak M *Lost in care* Gower, 1986.

5 Organisation of the fostering services

One of the factors which influenced the choice of project authorities was the way in which their foster care services were organised. We were interested to see whether any conclusions could be drawn about the effectiveness of their service when linked with material from our data base.

It must be acknowledged from the outset that any such relationship is extremely complex, and justifies a far more intensive analysis than our project resources allowed. Yet despite its limitations, the study provided a unique opportunity to consider organisational issues, which we hope will be explored further by other researchers. For our part, we have sought to describe and assess issues surrounding structure, believing that there are strengths and weaknesses in every organisational type. What follows is not about 'good' and 'bad' or 'right' and 'wrong' ways of providing a fostering service. Rather it is about advantages and disadvantages, potential and limitations.

The trend in many departments, since the mid-1970s in particular, has been to integrate fostering with selected children's services in specialised units. The most usual combination is fostering and adoption, but staff involved in the oversight of playgroups and childminders may also form part of the team. Fostering itself may be subdivided into various specialisms with one team dealing with mainstream work while another concentrates on teenage placements of the hard-to-place child. An alternative to locating specialists in a central unit may be the allocation of such posts to area teams. Sometimes one person specialises in fostering in an area office while in other instances a whole team will perform this function and be headed by a senior worker. If area-based fostering workers are outposted from a specialist unit, they may be managed by the unit or the area, or jointly by both. However, it is more usual for area posts to be part of the area structure and accountable to its hierarchy.

Despite the creation of many specialist posts, not all authorities have chosen to go down this road. North Thames is a good example of a department which has resisted any changes that would remove fostering from the control of the generic field social workers. Instead it has remained as part of the mixed caseload of area workers with a minimum of central office involvement. In essence, all the stages of the task from recruitment through to placement and foster parent liaison work are undertaken by area social workers in North Thames, whereas in our other five authorities some or all of the recruitment, assessment and linking of children with families is the responsibility of specialists. With a few exceptions, these are specialists who do not carry a caseload of children in care, although they do on occasions undertake direct work with children at the request of hard-pressed area staff.

From our project authorities there could not be seen to be any obvious relationship between type of authority and departmental fostering structure. For example, the two London boroughs had socio-economic similarities but were polar opposites in the way they organised their foster care. Furthermore, each of our metropolitan districts had more in common with one or other of the counties in this respect than with each other. Yet common throughout the six was a very real interest in organisational matters. In several places staff expressed the view that their system was not yet 'right' and others alluded to the difficulty of obtaining information and guidance on organisational matters. Those who had set out to explore this issue had mainly done so in an ad hoc manner, for example by visiting neighbouring authorities, or by visiting a department in which they happened to know people.

Of course, choice could not be freely determined. Usually the fostering service was expected to fit in with the style of organisation of the department as a whole and its philosophy. For example, localisation of service seemed to fit uneasily with specialism at the centre as very small neighbourhood teams usually require each social worker to operate as a generalist rather than a specialist. Yet any aspect of a department's work is shaped by many factors, and fostering is no exception. However stringent 'organisation' seemed to be, we were looking at a complex web of factors which shaped the service in each of the six authorities and perhaps accounted for the considerable differences between them. In an attempt to clarify the issues and highlight some of the differences, we tried to focus on the following specific aspects of the fostering and adoption structure in each authority.

- The existence of a central unit or adviser and role expectations.
- The existence and position in the authority of specialist staff and the range of their responsibilities.
- The provision of specialist schemes for placement of specific groups.
- The mechanism for approval of substitute families and the establishment of panels.
- The way in which adoption work was carried out.

Table 5.1

Structure of adoption and foster care services

	City	District	Midshire
1 Adoption service	Separate central unit which arranges all infant placements & advises foster parent adoptions.	Central adoption & fostering unit does all the adoption work.	Central adoption unit which arranges all infant placements. The PO Adoption also co-ordinates all long-term foster placements.
2 Specialist workers for foster care?	Yes, but fewer than one per area. Nominated area S.W. for short-term resources.	Yes. Within central unit only.	Yes. Fostering team for each division headed by senior.
3 Main tasks of specialist foster care workers	To recruit & assess families for long-term children & offer post-placement support.	Recruitment of all families & assessment of families for adolescents & advice & support for under-11s.	Recruitment, assessment, approval & general support of foster families.
4 Panels for foster home approval?	None. Approval of foster homes carried out by area managers.	Central panel for children.	Panels in divisions.
5 Special schemes	None.	None during project but under discussion.	Teen scheme began toward end of project.

The advantages and disadvantages of specialism

The six very different departments in which we conducted the fieldwork for the project provided an ideal opportunity to explore the issue of specialisation. We approached the topic in two ways. Firstly, we sought the views of workers in the departments on whether or not it was beneficial to have specialists undertaking aspects of the fostering task. We also raised the issue of where such posts should be located geographically in order to achieve maximum efficiency. Secondly, we

County	North Thames	South Thames
Most adoption service provided within divisions but carried out by specialist worker. Central Family Finders scheme for 'hard to place'.	Carried out by generic workers in area teams with reference to central specialists as necessary.	Infant adoptive placements referred to local adoption agency. Older children placed by central fostering & adoption unit.
Yes. Specialists within divisions plus staff in central Family Finders & Teen Care schemes.	No. Central specialists have advisory role only.	Yes. Large central unit (see 1), but some posts joint with areas.
Homefinding for some children (see above) & advice/ support base for area S.W.s.	Central staff are responsible for co-ordination & development of policy & practice.	Homefinding & assessment & support of families.
Central panels for approval of all applications.	Approval in areas. Arrangements vary between areas.	Six panels organised centrally.
Teen scheme & Family Finders scheme for children with special needs.	None.	Teen scheme.

71

considered the findings from our data in the light of departmental organisation. Did departments seem to have more 'successful' placements if they employed specialist staff? Were any other differences evident that could be linked to the presence or absence of specialist workers? We did not feel that we had been able to explore this important topic as deeply as would be desirable. Nor, as the following chapters will show, did we find clear-cut links between organisation and outcome. Nevertheless, we hope that the comments and findings will aid workers when reflecting on their own departmental organisation and perhaps encourage other researchers to explore the topic more fully.

From interviews with selected people in each department it was possible to draw together a number of commonly held views about specialisation, covering both advantages and disadvantages.

Advantages
Effectiveness
The most prevalent theme was the *effectiveness* of specialists in achieving placements. Time and again it was stated that social workers who were trying to manage a demanding caseload could not find the time to undertake the often all-consuming task of recruiting, preparing and supporting foster parents. Indeed, direct work with children who had been identified for fostering placement also lost out to the needs of children at risk and other onerous responsibilities.

Expertise
Specialists were seen as having more expertise in child placement than their non-specialist colleagues for the obvious reason that they were carrying out this work all the time. This was felt to benefit colleagues as well as clients as the specialists could give advice on specific issues and keep the department up to date generally on matters relating to substitute family care.

In all the project authorities there was evidence of increasing effort to plan for children and where there was a reasonable number of specialists, they were able to attend some planning meetings and could make a useful contribution.

Identification of key people
It was thought that specialism provided a useful focus within a

department which helped others to identify people to assist on particular issues. For example, it may help other agencies who are seeking a placement to liaise more effectively, or enable contacts such as those with the media to be made quickly and efficiently.

Uniformity and economies of scale
Despite the trend in many departments towards a service which is closer to the community and meeting local needs, uniformity across area boundaries was also thought to be important. Several people touched on the difficulty of presenting a coherent and comparable service across areas if the structure did not include specialists. A particular example of this is resource sharing which it was felt required effective and frequent communication between people who were well informed about children and families on referral. This sharing of resources also benefited from an authority-wide perspective which helped to ensure that the needs of children were seen as more important than keeping a family without a placement so that they could be available should a need arise in the area that had approved them.

On a more general note, departments with specialists considered themselves more effective due to economy of scale. Posters and leaflets could be drawn up for the whole department thus avoiding numerous local initiatives which multiply aspects of the work. North Thames, where specialism was consistently avoided, was a good example of how difficult it can be to develop authority-wide information and resources. During the period of our fieldwork they were still grappling with producing basic tools such as fostering leaflets and posters.

Data collection
Departments with specialist staff seemed to find it easier to monitor their work and to provide statistical information.

These were the main benefits which staff associated with specialism. But not all the commments were positive, and both the specialists and non-specialists also mentioned disadvantages. These can be summarised as follows:

Disadvantages
Relationships with areas
The relationship between specialists and area social workers con-

73

sistently arose as the most problematic issue. Rightly or wrongly, specialists tended to be viewed as an elite carrying out tasks which were a 'soft option' in comparison to colleagues undertaking a wide range of statutory responsibilities. The situation was often more tense if specialists functioned from a separate unit rather than an area team location. It was equivalent in area eyes to an ivory tower. Specialists found this aspect of their situation decidedly fraught, too. One described her unit's relationship with area workers as 'like treading on eggshells'. Specialists also felt frustrated on occasions by their powerlessness. As their posts were usually of an advisory nature they often found themselves used selectively rather than appropriately. They had no line management responsibility in relation to area staff and therefore could not determine how, when or by whom work was carried out.

Distance from local need

Another criticism of specialist units was their lack of appreciation of local needs. This represents the converse side of the argument for uniformity, for although a unit may carry forward authority-wide issues as discussed earlier, this can be at the expense of local variation. In small authorities without major internal differences (for example, in socio-economic characteristics) this may not be particularly significant. However, in large and diverse authorities it may be very difficult to treat the authority as a single entity. Furthermore, local people may respond more readily to a community-based approach with which they can identify, as seems to happen in North Thames.

Monopoly of knowledge and expertise

A further criticism of specialism was that knowledge was developed and shared (as discussed earlier) but that it was retained rather than communicated to non-specialist colleagues. This monopoly of knowledge was also seen as unhelpful to clients who may prefer to deal with one social worker who is involved in every aspect of the task, e.g. finding foster parents for their child as well as having statutory responsibility for his or her case.

The location of specialist posts

Can the disadvantages of specialism described above be overcome if staff are located in area offices rather than a central unit? Are joint posts shared between areas and a specialist unit advantageous? To what extent can 'informal' linking with areas prove effective, and under what circumstances? Situating specialists in area teams has certain distinct advantages over the separate specialist unit. It can overcome many problems of communication, lessening the 'them and us' issue as described earlier as well as the feeling that local needs and pressures are not appreciated. However, the position of being the only specialist in an area was not a particularly enviable one. Complaints were made about having as line managers seniors who knew little about the work and who failed to protect staff from inappropriate referrals and requests from colleagues. Furthermore, an individual specialist is particularly vulnerable to the way in which the area hierarchy perceives his or her role. Some specialists were expected to undertake duty enquiries, for example, whereas in a neighbouring office a mile or two away this would be unthinkable. Although differences in local demands sometimes justifies such variation, the more usual explanation was that assumptions were made when the post was created which remained unchallenged as the years went by. We were constantly amazed by the extent to which areas differed and the part that tradition and personalities played within each of our departments. The result for the specialist staff was often a feeling of isolation. They did not feel part of the area team nor could they completely identify with their opposite numbers in other parts of the authority.

From our observations and the comments made to us, it would appear that social workers who function as part of an area based specialist team are in many ways in a more satisfactory position. They have the support of colleagues doing the same job and a specialist senior to offer supervision and guidance. However, it is not always feasible for a department to institute specialist teams particularly if it is small and employs relatively few staff, or if it has opted for service delivery via tiny but numerous neighbourhood offices.

A compromise between the specialist unit and area based specialist is the joint post. This allows a worker to have the proverbial 'foot in both camps' and when it works well can offer the best of both worlds – or can it? In South Thames, where a number of joint posts existed, both the positives and the negatives of such an arrangement were stressed. On the positive side joint appointments helped bridge the gap that can distance area offices from specialised units, and facilitate communication. But they can also leave the worker in a limbo with a divided role and set of allegiences. As soon as a difference of opinion arises between centre and area the worker has to either take sides or appear neutral and relationships can easily suffer. Another area of vulnerability seems to be the management and supervision of workers in joint posts. Perhaps the most difficult situation for all concerned is when area managers and senior staff in specialist units are at variance with each other with the worker caught somewhere in the middle. Yet even if relationships are good, the proportion of time spent in liaising with managers is likely to be greater in total for a shared post, and three way meetings, involving the senior from the area, and from the centre as well as the worker may also be considered necessary. This is just one aspect of the much wider issue of time management which befalls anyone doing what is in effect two part-time jobs, and can easily result in one task eating into the time allocated for the other, coupled with the feeling that one is never in the right place at the right time.

Some authorities, such as District, chose to develop a specialist section or unit but to link a worker with an area office so that he or she could be a regular presence and offer a surgery for problem cases, attend team meetings, participate in reviews and panels and generally relay the views and needs of the area to the centre and vice versa. Obviously such an arrangement can facilitate good working relationships and aid communication, but there can be drawbacks of both a practical and professional nature. It seems that informal links can work well in small authorities where geographical distances are limited. It is far less feasible to be a regular presence, say, in a large county as so much time would be spent travelling. Professionally it can also be taxing to be involved informally as the danger is that one is drawn into situations too late or inappropriately and, as in other posts which do not carry responsibility for line management, advice may be ignored.

Conclusions

Earlier in this section we stated that what followed was not about 'good' and 'bad' or 'right' and 'wrong' ways of providing a fostering service. By the time the descriptive part of the study was completed, we were more than ever convinced that structural changes do not necessarily – or even usually – solve problems. It is a mirage to think that a re-organisation will deal with difficulties over practice or policy.

Each of our project authorities gave credence to the view that what works in one department will not necessarily work in another, and that every organisational type has strengths as well as weaknesses. We were constantly reminded of the tension of, on the one hand, trying to disperse skills, knowledge and responsibility as widely as possible and as close to the community as possible, while, on the other hand, risking the neglect of highly complex, delicate and time-consuming tasks which can be crowded out if there are no specialists with a specific brief and interest to ensure they are accomplished. As these tasks are to do with the well-being of children in care and their families, consequences can be very serious indeed.

6 Foster family placements

In this chapter we raise many of the same issues as before but focus specifically on foster placements. The project has provided information on 4615 foster placements. In 819 cases we only have information about the ending because the placement had started before the project began – sometimes many years before, sometimes only a few weeks earlier. There were 2735 foster placements which began and ended during our two years of monitoring and 1061 placements which started and were continuing when the project finished. So we have 3796 foster starts and 3554 ends distributed like this:

$$\rangle - - \frac{819}{-\,-\,-} - - \rbrack$$

$$\lbrack - - - - \frac{2735}{-\,-\,-} - - - - \rbrack .$$

$$\lbrack - - - - \frac{1061}{-\,-\,-} - - - - \rightarrow$$

Further enquiries, after data collection was over, revealed another 67 endings which had not been notified. But it still seems that in our six authorities there were slightly more children in foster homes at the end of the project than there had been at the beginning. This is in line with recent trends.

In considering the data, it is important to bear in mind that the nature of our sample excludes stable long-term placements where no change occurred during the course of the project. The exclusion of these ongoing placements has the effect of accentuating the number of young children who have very short periods in foster care. Great caution also has to be exercised in talking of 'success' or 'breakdown' rates especially if these are to be compared with other studies.

The general picture
Perhaps one's most immediate reaction from studying the project data

is how different it all seems from what is being discussed at child care conferences and written about in professional journals. Inevitably papers and articles tend to focus on new developments and the last few years have seen much emphasis on task-centred foster care and specialist schemes for adolescents. Long-term fostering has gone out of fashion and remarkably little attention has ever been paid to short-stay fostering.

Our findings make it possible to compare theory with reality. They offer a salutary reminder that the day to day, bread and butter work of fostering is still the placement of young children needing care for a brief period during a family crisis or to give relief to their hard-pressed parents.

Age and placement aims

Age at placement is important because it reveals the pattern of the foster care service and because of the strong association of age at placement and placement outcome. Two questions need to be considered. First, what proportion of placements in each age group are foster placements? Second, what is the age distribution of children going into foster homes?

The pie charts in Chapter 3 showed how the proportion of children being placed in foster homes drops rapidly with increasing age. In spite of current emphasis on family care, most adolescents still go into residential establishments of some sort.

The percentage of teenage placements in foster homes varied considerably in our six authorities. It was highest in the two which had specialist fostering schemes for adolescents, but even in these it did not reach 25 per cent. Specialist placements accounted for 22 per cent of teenage foster placements but made up only three per cent of all teenage in-care placements. Clearly there is a long way to go before specialist fostering plays a major part in provision for adolescents.

Table 6.1 sets out the age pattern of foster placements for the whole group and by authority. It shows that half (51%) of all the foster placements made during the project were of children under five years old, 26 per cent were aged five to ten and only 23 per cent (854 children) were of secondary school age. It also shows up the large differences in the age patterns of the foster placements made by each authority. Whereas almost two-thirds of District's foster placements were pre-schoolers, only two out of five of South Thames' foster

Table 6.1

Ages of children being placed in foster homes, by authority

	All	City	District	Mid-shire	County	North Thames	South Thames
N =	3796	1221	190	861	695	494	335
0–4 (N = 1937)	51%	56%	65%	48%	51%	48%	39%
5–10 (N = 1005)	26%	28%	20%	28%	18%	35%	24%
11+ (N = 854)	23%	16%	15%	24%	31%	17%	37%

Table 6.2

Age and primary aim at placement start

	All	0–4	5–10	11+
N =	3796	1937	1005	854
Temporary care	39%	46%	46%	15%
Emergency/roof	12%	11%	12%	13%
Task-centred	34%	34%	26%	43%
Care & upbringing	13%	7%	14%	26%
Other (including adoption & remand	2%	2%	2%	3%

placements were in this youngest age group. In fact, South Thames placed almost as many adolescents as pre-schoolers. This is more than twice as high a proportion as in either City, District or North Thames.

Age is also closely related to placement aims. In Table 6.2, the task-centred aims of treatment, assessment, preparation for long-term placement and bridge to independence have been grouped together in order to make comparisons easier.

Several interesting points emerge from a detailed look at these placement aims. Getting on for half (46%) of all foster placements for the under 11s were for temporary care. And if temporary care and 'emergency roof over head' placements are put together, they account for 51 per cent of all foster placements made by the project authorities.

Task-centred placements made up a third of all placements and 43 per cent of placements of teenagers. However, it is important to realise that 43 per cent of 854 teenage placements is 362 while 34 per cent of the much larger number of pre-school placements is 663. So, though task-centred fostering is more often thought of in connection with adolescents, we found that in fact there were more task-centred placements of young children. This has implications for the selection, training and support of foster parents.

The situation is reversed when we look at care and upbringing placements. It might be expected that these would most often involve young children but instead we find 225 (26%) of these placements in the 11+ age group, compared with only 144 (7%) of the under-five age group. These figures can be partly explained by the large proportion of temporary care placements for young children (which makes the proportion of care and upbringing placements look small), and partly by the current feeling that long-term foster care is an inappropriate placement for children of this age. But it also highlights the considerable number of adolescents in need of long-term care and nurture in a family setting. The difficulty of providing this will become apparent when we look at foster home outcomes in relation to age at placement.

Aims and expected length
Another insight to emerge was the realisation that the aim of the placement has to be set alongside its expected length before foster care patterns can be properly understood.

In the early days of the child care service, it was perfectly appropriate to make a simple division between short-term and long-term fostering. Both were intended to provide 'care' with no expectation that foster parents would also be asked to fulfil specific additional tasks such as assessment or treatment. Fostering was usually seen as appropriate for young children only, and placements planned to last for intermediate periods of time were rather rare. It is not too much of a simplification to say that children either left within six to eight weeks or they remained in care and the foster placement was expected to last indefinitely.

The development of task-centred fostering has coincided with the growth of the concept of intermediate-length foster care and there has been a tendency to assume that placements expected to last for between two months and two years are task-focused whereas short-term (less than two months) or long-term placements (three years or more) are not. We found that although the majority of short-term placements are for temporary or emergency care and most really long-term placements are for care and upbringing, there is nevertheless a great deal of overlap.

Table 6.3

Aim and expected length of foster placements

		< 4 weeks	4–7 weeks	2–66 months	mths– 2 years	3 + years	Uncer- tain/NK
N =	3796	1397	438	798	287	356	520
% row	100%	37%	12%	21%	8%	9%	13%
Temporary care	1471						
	100%	72%	12%	7%	1%	–	8%
Emergency/roof	446						
	100%	41%	12%	21%	2%	–	24%
Assessment	402						
	100%	11%	16%	40%	8%	–	25%
Treatment	299						
	100%	24%	13%	37%	11%	1%	14%
Bridge to independence	140						
	100%	–	4%	16%	61%	10%	9%
Care & upbringing	512						
	100%	1%	1%	14%	12%	53%	19%
Preparation long-term placement	440						
	100%	5%	20%	53%	11%	–	11%
Other (including adoption)	86						
	100%	13%	4%	2%	6%	63%	12%

Table 6.3 shows that 23 per cent of emergency/roof over head placements are expected to exceed seven weeks in duration. The wide range of purposes for which short-term placements are used is also evident. No fewer than 37 per cent of placements where the primary aim is treatment are expected to be short-term as are 27 per cent of assessment placements. It is also worth noting that care and upbringing is by no means synonymous with long-term, for 28 per cent of these placements are not expected to last beyond two years.

The importance of looking at aim in relation to length becomes evident when one starts to analyse outcomes. Some aims are more difficult to achieve than others, irrespective of their expected duration. It can therefore be potentially misleading to suggest that short-term or longer term placements are more or less likely to be 'successful' without also specifying their aims. This may explain what otherwise seem unaccountable differences in the breakdown rates of short-term placements which have been reported from neighbouring authorities (for example, Devon in 1981,[1] and Avon[2]). It may be that they use their short-term foster homes for different purposes.

We found that aims varied considerably between authorities. Sometimes this seemed to be linked with authority policies. (For example, North Thames made heavy use of temporary care placements as a way of supporting families in times of stress.) Other differences in aim were much harder to explain. For instance, there seemed to be no obvious reason why South Thames should have had an above average number of foster placements where the aim was treatment, while Midshire was above average for assessment.

Beginnings, emergencies and choice
Social work textbooks are apt to write about foster placements as if they are either new admissions or transfers from children's homes after a period of introduction. In our sample, 59 per cent of foster placements were from home, 17 per cent from another foster home, 10 per cent from a residential establishment and 14 per cent from some other living situations. Young children mostly came from home but one in three teenagers moved to a foster home from residential care and another 18 per cent were changing foster homes.

'Emergencies' loom large in foster care. Seventy-two percent of all admission placements to foster homes were said by the child's social worker to be of an emergency nature although only a minority of these

83

were completely new referrals. 'Emergency' is a word used rather loosely in social services departments. One is reminded of the social worker who said she was expecting to do an emergency placement in three weeks' time.

Moves between placements can also be 'emergencies' and 35 per cent of foster placements of children already in care were coded as such. These proportions seem very high and affect all age groups, but they accord with the findings of other researchers, for example, Packman[3] and Millham,[4] who report on the crisis nature of many admissions and moves.

We had hoped to be able to trace the effect of emergencies on outcomes, but it proved to be too subtle a concept for our data which are essentially quantitative rather than qualitative. The majority of emergency foster placements are for temporary care or 'roof over head' and, as we shall see, these usually last and meet their aims reasonably well. Placements with the aims which are harder to achieve (for example, treatment, bridge to independence or care and upbringing) are the least likely to be emergencies. This accounts for the otherwise surprising finding that planned placements failed to last as needed more often than emergency placements.

Pressure on placement resources of all kinds, and shortage of foster homes in particular, seem to be recurrent themes at social work gatherings and in professional journals. Because of this and the potentially damaging effect of unsuitable placements, our questionnaires included the topics of choice and appropriateness. Unfortunately, the results are not particularly illuminating. This is partly because lack of choice may be due either to scarcity of homes or to the choice being made by others either in the department or by a court. Nor does limitation on choice necessarily mean that the placement used is considered unsuitable. What does come through clearly from our data is that social workers rather seldom feel that they have sufficient choice, but they even less often rate the suitability of the foster home as 'doubtful' or 'inappropriate'. We are not sure how to interpret this.

Moves and discharges
Of the 3554 foster home endings in our project sample, 43 per cent were moves within the care system. More than one in every three foster home endings for the under 11s was a move to another placement and teenagers moved still more often. However, only a quarter of all the

foster home endings we studied were specifically stated to be 'unplanned' moves and although, as explained in Chapter I, we think this is probably an under-estimate, moves are not necessarily detrimental. Many placements have aims which inevitably include a move. Examples are: preparing a child for a long-term placement, or assessing needs as part of a planning process. Other positive moves are returning home on trial (16 per cent of all moves), or moving to independent living (2%). There were only a handful of clearly detrimental moves, such as transfer from a foster home into a penal establishment, or into a bed and breakfast hotel.

Other researchers[4,5] have commented on the flow of former foster children into residential establishments. In our sample there were more than twice as many moves into other foster homes (818) as into residential care (386). But it is interesting to note that whereas more than two-thirds of the moves to other foster homes were said to be part of the plan, nearly three-quarters of the moves to residential care were definitely unplanned and due to the premature ending of the foster placement.

Four out of every five discharges from foster homes occurred when the child returned home. There were 96 discharges on the making of an adoption or custodianship order and 185 young people in foster homes graduated out of the care system at 18. This group of 185 makes up less than ten per cent of all foster discharges over the two year period and is a reminder that few children who come into care grow up to adulthood in a foster family. This finding is reinforced by our data on length of placement. Overall, only six per cent of foster home placements had lasted more than five years, though this rose to 32 per cent of those who were in the 16+ age group at placement end.

Length, drift and premature endings
We have already seen that most foster placements were expected to be brief and this is indeed what happened. Nearly one placement in five (19%) lasted less than a week and more than half (55%) ended in less than two months. Just over one in three (36%) were of intermediate length (two months to two years) and only ten per cent had lasted over three years.

What has to be borne in mind when studying placement lengths is that they include cases which have ended prematurely and others that have lasted much longer than originally expected as well as those which ended as planned. The social workers' replies to the question on whether the placement had lasted according to plan show that for older children, premature endings were much more usual than placements which went on beyond the expected time span. Youngsters in their mid-teens were specially vulnerable. Pre-school and primary children's placements were almost as likely to turn into a longer stay as to end sooner than originally expected. For the whole group, about half the foster placements were said to have lasted as planned, a quarter had not and 15 per cent lasted longer. In the remaining ten per cent there had been no plan about the placement's duration.

Table 6.4

Whether placement lasted as planned, by age

	All	0–4	5–10	11–13	14–15	16+
N =	3554	1626	866	332	310	420
Lasted as long as planned	49%	55%	52%	30%	24%	50%
Did not last as long as planned	26%	18%	20%	41%	59%	35%
Lasted longer than planned	15%	17%	16%	16%	10%	8%
Not applicable – no plan	10%	9%	11%	13%	7%	7%
NK	–	–	1%	–	1%	–

Extended stays and premature endings can both occur for either negative or positive reasons. Drift in foster placements does not seem to be happening on any large scale. There were only 54 foster placements which started in Year 1 and had seriously exceeded their expected duration when the project ended. No doubt some of these situations were perfectly satisfactory. However, there was a preponderance of younger children among the 54 'over-stayers'. This is rather worrying because of the importance for them of the passage of time.

Although it is interesting and useful to know what proportion of placements last as planned, a more important question is whether they last as long as needed. The overall answer is quite positive with 66 per cent of placements having lasted as long as the children needed them. However, once again there is a steady rise across the age bands in the proportion of placements not lasting as needed (0–4, 16%; 5–10, 20%; 11+, 40%). By cross-tabulating the answers to these questions we discover that of 922 placements which did not go on as long as planned, 254 (28%), had nevertheless lasted as long as needed. Conversely, 165 of the 843 that had not gone on as long as the child needed, had lasted as long or even longer than planned (20%). But probably the most useful information is that set out in Table 6.5. This shows that getting on for half the foster placement endings (45%) were said to have lasted both as long as planned and as long as needed while fewer than one in five (17%) had failed to meet either the social work plan or the child's needs.

Table 6.5

How placements lasted

		Lasted as planned	Not as long as planned	Longer than planned	Not applicable/NK
N = 3554		1738	922	535	359
% = % of all foster endings		49%	26%	15%	10%
Lasted as needed	2361	1582	254	289	236
	66%	45%	7%	8%	7%
Did not last	843	116	608	49	70
as needed	24%	3%	17%	1%	2%
Lasted too long	329	33	59	197	40
	9%	1%	2%	6%	1%
NK	21	7	1	–	13
	–	–	–	–	–

Problems in the placement
Immediately following the question about the circumstances of placement ending, social workers were asked to indicate whether any of a list of problems had occurred during the placement. More than one problem could be coded. The main object was to find out how often particular difficulties had arisen, but the responses proved to be a

87

useful way of explaining what had been going on and the reasons for some social worker ratings.

The most frequently noted problem was 'placement satisfactory at first, problems later'. This was coded for ten per cent of placements which ended when the child was under 11 and for 36 per cent of placement endings of adolescents (18 per cent overall). Sometimes this coding was associated with the child or young person returning home or moving to independent living, but in 70 per cent of these cases this coding was linked with a move to another, in-care placement. The frequency of this response among adolescent placements prompts speculation about the level of social work support to the foster home and whether it was maintained at a sufficiently high level in placements which at first appeared to be proceeding satisfactorily. It also reinforces the findings of other researchers that social workers may not be aware of the build-up of problems in a placement (for example, Berridge and Cleaver's[6] finding that in over a quarter of long-term foster placements which broke down, social workers had thought that all was well).

The next most usual problem was 'child's behaviour unacceptable to caregivers'. This was noted in 28 per cent of adolescent foster home endings but for only six per cent of endings for younger children (13 per cent overall). The behaviour problems most likely to be associated with this response were: attention seeking, general unmanageability, aggression/temper and stealing. It is interesting, however, that even the most frequently mentioned problem (attention seeking) was not noted in as many as a third of the cases where the child's behaviour was unacceptable.

In our study of long-term foster care,[7] we found major differences between the accounts of foster children's behaviour given by their foster parents and what was recorded on social work files. There was strong evidence that foster parents try to manage on their own, do not always inform social workers about the children's behaviour problems and complain that when they do ask for advice and help social workers cannot offer much support.[8] It therefore seems likely that behaviour problems are considerably under-reported in the current project but they are nevertheless still a major reason for placement disruption. Our data show that in getting on for two thirds of cases where teenagers were having an unplanned move from a foster home to a residential establishment or to another foster home, their behaviour was said to have been unacceptable to their foster parents. Aldgate and Hawley,[9] in their study of fostering disruptions, report a high incidence of behaviour problems. They say: 'One of the main causes of trouble was the behaviour of children, which was tolerated at first but gradually became completely unacceptable.' Overall, seven per cent of foster placements ended because an 'unexpected event in the foster family caused disruption'. This was the cause of 12 per cent of teenage foster endings but of only 5 per cent of endings of children aged under 11. Two points seem particularly noteworthy about these cases. The first is that in a third of them the social worker also coded that the child's behaviour had been unacceptable. One cannot help wondering how often some event in the foster home was used as an 'easier' reason for requesting the child's removal.

The second point to note is that the percentage of placements which disrupted because of some unforeseen event in the foster family, varied between authorities as well as between children's age groups. No less than 17 per cent of Midshire's teenage foster placement endings had this coding compared with only six per cent in South Thames.

It was encouraging to find that problems with the children's own families were not widespread. There were only 135 out of the 3554 endings (4%), where the parents were said to have withdrawn their child against advice and 211 cases (6%), where parents were considered to have caused difficulties. (In 41 cases both these problems were coded so there were just nine per cent of foster placements where relationships with parents had been a problem.)

To conclude this section, we should note that 110 foster placements (3%) ended because a court ordered a change of plan or change of placement. Such orders were just as likely to apply to younger children as to adolescents.

Lasting and helpfulness
Whether or not a foster placement lasts as required has been the main touchstone against which success or failure has traditionally been measured. Yet social workers are aware that a foster placement may last a long time but still fail to meet many of the child's needs, while placements that do not last as long as needed can sometimes be truly said to have done a lot of good. For instance, a placement may have enabled a child's personality and needs to be so much better understood that a more suitable foster family can be selected and a

change of placement beneficially accomplished.

Overall, 28 per cent of foster endings that had not lasted as long as needed were nevertheless rated as 'very helpful'. What has been described as social workers' 'rule of optimism' may have been at work here. However, even in situations which can only be accurately described as 'unsuccessful', many of the original aims of placement may have been met quite adequately. This can happen, for example, when a 'care and upbringing' placement which has been stable for many years falls apart in the difficult years of adolescence, and the youngster moves out prematurely to independent living.

It is important to remember that this project's results are based on the perceptions of the social workers and do not include the views of the young people or caregivers. Moreover, the angle from which the social workers approach the questions will have had a profound influence on their responses. To draw very fine distinctions on the basis of subjective responses would be potentially very dangerous. Yet no overview of foster care outcomes would be complete without an attempt to report on whether these placements were perceived by those responsible as having been helpful to the children and young people who experienced them.

Looking across the wide spectrum of endings we can see that social workers rated foster placements very highly in terms of helpfulness to children. Nearly half of all endings received the highest rating 'very helpful', with a further third rated 'fairly helpful'.

Table 6.6

Social workers' rating on the helpfulness of the placement

	N = 3554	100%
Very helpful	1645	46%
Fairly helpful	1223	34%
Not very helpful	325	9%
Unhelpful	100	3%
Can't say	238	7%
NK	23	1%

There was no overall difference in ratings of placements of boys and girls and there was remarkably little difference between age groups. Placements which ended when young people were in their teens were almost as likely to be considered 'helpful' as were placement endings of younger children. The single exception was that placements of adolescent girls were the least likely to be perceived as 'very helpful'. This similarity between age groups is somewhat perplexing because teenage endings got lower ratings for achieving their aims and were much more often reported as having failed to last as long as needed. The best explanation for this seems to be that, as we shall see below, teenage placements tend to have complex aims which are hard to achieve and these placements are also hard to sustain. The young person may have to move on before the aim has been achieved but is felt to have benefited in other ways.

Achieving aims
At first sight the overall figures of aims achieved seem very encouraging. Seventy-five per cent of all foster placements were rated as having achieved their aims fully (48%), or 'in most respects' (27%). However, unlike the helpfulness ratings there is a marked age difference here with 80 per cent of placements of the under 11s achieving their aims at least in most respects while this rating was achieved in only 64 per cent of endings for children aged 11+.

Closer study reveals that it is not only age that is important in determining outcome but the inter-relationship of age and aim which was discussed briefly in Chapter 4. It is not just that teenagers can be difficult for foster parents to handle or to live with.In looking at foster placement outcomes, we have to remember that a much higher proportion of teenagers have placement aims which are difficult to achieve. This is a complicated issue both to tease out and to explain because age seems to affect some aims much more than others. It seems best to list the most usual aims with the percentages in which those aims were achieved and then to consider each in turn. A glance at the table shows that the 'easiest' aim – temporary care – was achieved almost twice as frequently as the most difficult aim – treatment.

We have already noted that more than half the placements of young children were for temporary care and now find that this less complex aim was achieved in at least most respects for 88 per cent. Adolescent placements for temporary care were almost equally successful (85%)

91

Table 6.7

Percentage of foster placements in which aims were achieved fully or in most respect, by age

N = 3554   % = % achieved fully or in most respects

Aim	All ages	0–10	11+
Temporary care	88%	88%	85%
Emergency/roof	83%	88%	71%
Prep.l.t. placement	79%	83%	50%
Assessment	57%	63%	36%
Treatment	46%	46%	45%
Bridge to independence	53%	–	53%
Care & upbringing	66%	63%	66%

but few in number – only 119 compared to the 1303 for the under 11s.

Preparation for long-term placement was also used mainly for younger children and in these cases usually met its aims (83%). However, when this was the aim in an 11 + placement it was much less often achieved (50%). There was a similar but less extreme dip in the achievement rating for emergency/roof over head placements. Here the range was 88 per cent fully or mostly achieved for under 11s and 71 per cent for over 11s.

When it comes to treatment and assessment, the findings are perplexing. Both are difficult aims to achieve at any age, being achieved fully or mostly for just over half (57%) of all assessment placements and less than half (46%) of treatment placements. But whereas age evidently has a strong effect on achieving the aim of assessment, it seems to have none at all on treatment. The aim of assessment was achieved in 63 per cent of cases where the child was aged under 11 but only 36 per cent of cases of those aged 11 +.The equivalent figures for placements with a treatment aim are 46 per cent and 45 per cent.

Our data provide insufficient detail to explain these differences. It may be that when treatment is the aim in cases of younger children, it is usually directed at their parents and that it is as difficult to achieve successful treatment for them as for the adolescents in care. But this can only be conjecture.

It is also hard to understand why, in the project authorities, assessment of teenagers in foster homes should be so unsuccessful in meeting their aims, especially when some other authorities have special assessment foster homes for difficult adolescents that appear to work very well. It has been suggested that part of the problem may be lack of a planned and explicit focus on assessment so that foster parents are not clear about what needs to be done. Another suggestion is that social workers may have unrealistic hopes that assessment will produce not just a plan but a solution and then feel that the aim has not been achieved when this does not happen. Whatever the reason, the results for adolescent foster home assessments and for treatment placements for all age groups seem to be worryingly low even when the very real difficulties of the task are taken into account.

Bridge to independence is, of course, only relevant for older teenagers. It, too, is a difficult aim and was fully or mostly achieved in only 53 per cent of foster placements.

Care and upbringing appears to be somewhat easier. This aim had been fully or mostly achieved in 66 per cent of foster placement endings. However, the apparent similarity between older and younger age groups is misleading. Early endings in what should often have been long-term placements are not very likely to have achieved their aims. Younger children therefore appear to be relatively unsuccessful. In the next chapter on long-term fostering, we shall see that age does have a profound effect. When children are older at placement start, breakdowns are far more frequent. But if one looks at age at ending and aim achieved, there seems to be almost no difference between age groups.

Lasting
The importance of providing and maintaining a placement that can last as long as the child needs it is as obvious as it is central. Not lasting as needed is not synonymous with foster home breakdown, but is always a crucial component of breakdown.

We can look across the whole range of foster home endings and see that 24 per cent are said not to have lasted as needed. But this masks a wide range of different outcomes in which age and aim are crucial factors. It is not possible to show the complex inter-relationships of age, aim and length on a single table, but it may help to set out in graphic form the proportion of placements that had not lasted as needed according to the aim of placement and the age of the child. Figure 6.1 does this and shows how the proportion of premature endings increases with increasing difficulty of the aim though the pattern is uneven because of variations by age group.

Figure 6.1
Percentage of foster placements that did not last as needed, by aim and age

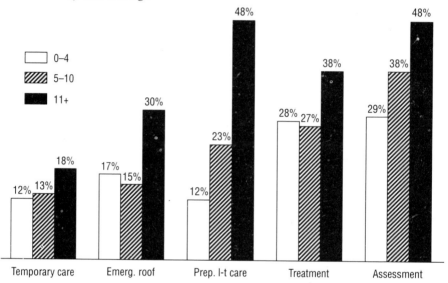

This figure also deals with age. It shows that within each aim, adolescents always have a higher percentage of premature endings than do the younger children. The increase from pre-schoolers to the 11 + group varies from a small rise of six per cent (temporary care), to a huge jump of 36 per cent (preparation for long-term placement). Sometimes the rise is steady. Sometimes there is a dip for the five to ten age group, but the increased difficulty of sustaining teenagers in their foster placements is all too clear.

Bridge to independence placements are excluded from this figure because they only concern adolescents but 44 per cent of them did not last as needed. Care and upbringing placements are also excluded because, as already explained, endings of long-term placements are distorted in the lower age bands in tables based on age at placement ending. Of the care and upbringing placements which ended when the child was aged 11 +, 42 per cent were said not to have lasted as long as needed.

With these patterns in mind, it may help to consider our findings about each aim in turn.

Temporary care placements had not only achieved their aims, they had usually lasted as long as needed. Overall only 13 per cent did not last, and this only rises to 18 per cent for teenagers.

Emergency holding care, with the descriptive by-line 'roof over head', clearly falls into the short-term category and in some respects it might be thought right to group it together with temporary care. However, emergency 'holding' placements are differentiated both by their inherent uncertainty, and because they are often a 'roof between two in-care placements rather than a refuge for the child who will return home as soon as the family crisis is over. One in five of 'emergency holding' endings was coded as not having lasted as long as needed, and for teenagers, 30 per cent of these brief placements failed to last compared with the 18 per cent of 'temporary care' placements for the same age-group.

Once again, the contrast between 'temporary care' and special purposes placements is stark even if expected. Overall, 31 per cent of treatment placements failed to last as needed and placements of younger children were not very much more successful – 28 per cent of their treatment placements did not last compared with 38 per cent for adolescents. Assessment placements, too, had many premature endings. Nearly a third of all assessment foster placements, and almost half of those where the child was a teenager, were said not to have lasted as long as needed.

'Preparation for long-term care' is another aim in the 'special purpose' category but it sounds a rather straightforward aim which one might expect would achieve fairly high ratings for lasting. The younger child placements with this aim did last well with only 12 per cent ending prematurely. (Indeed, 20 per cent of these placements were said to have lasted too long.) But, as Figure 6.1 shows, the 'did not last' group rises to 23 per cent for youngsters aged five to ten, and to 48 per cent of the foster placements intended to prepare adolescents for a long-term family. Perhaps the difficulty of recruiting long-term families for adolescents means that these preparation placements often need to go on for much longer than originally planned and this causes too much strain on either child or family or both.

'Successful' and 'unsuccessful' placements

Since the ratings 'successful' and 'unsuccessful' are based on whether or not a placement lasted as needed and whether the aims were achieved, they will obviously follow the patterns seen in previous sections. Temporary care is usually 'successful'. Task-focused placements do not fare so well. The rating is a crude measure and does not take into account whether or not the placement was considered helpful or how any of the parties immediately concerned felt about it.

Even with these points in mind and acknowledging that the standard being set may be considered fairly high, the ratings make sobering reading. The overall figure is quite encouraging. Sixty per cent of all foster endings were 'successful' and only 15 per cent 'unsuccessful'. However, this is because temporary care placements were not only highly 'successful' but also very numerous. They accounted for two-thirds of all the 'successes'. Placements where the aim had been adoption were also highly successful (83%) but few in number. Emergency/roof over head achieved a 64 per cent success rate and preparation for long-term placement just topped the half-way mark at 55 per cent. None of the other task-focused placements achieved a 50 per cent success rate and nor did care and upbringing. The scores were assessment 44 per cent, care and upbringing 43 per cent, bridge to independence 42 per cent and treatment 37 per cent.

When it comes to the 'unsuccessful' group, we find that 26 per cent of care and upbringing placements fall into this category as did 30 per cent of assessment placements and 34 per cent of those where the aim was bridge to independence. It is noteworthy that 49 per cent of the 'unsuccessful' placements concerned children aged 11+ at placement ending, although this age group accounts for only 30 per cent of foster home endings.

Differences between the overall 'success' rates in the six authorities are not quite great enough to be statistically significant but it may be useful to note that the higher the percentage of adolescents, the lower the 'success' rate.

Within particular age bands there are some bigger differences. Quite often these are explicable when considered in the context of each authority's policies and the way foster care is used. Thus, somewhat lower 'success' rates for the 11 + group in Midshire, County and South Thames can probably be linked with their higher rate of foster placements of teenagers. These authorities are almost certainly trying to foster more difficult young people than are the authorities with lower foster placement rates for adolescents. But there seems no such obvious reason for low success rates for the under-fives in the two London boroughs. (It is not due to their placing more ethnic minority children as Chapter 12 will show.) Nor are the lower than average 'success' rates among District's and County's foster placements of five to tens easily explained. The whole issue of comparisons between authorities is considered in the final section of this chapter.

Specialist fostering for teenagers

The sample
In view of the widespread professional interest in specialist family placement schemes for adolescents, it was somewhat surprising to find them in only two of our six authorities, County and South Thames. (A scheme was just starting in Midshire during the last few months of the project.) We wondered whether this meant that we had a distorted picture of teenage placements. There is no really accurate and up-to-date national information on this topic, but surveys by Thomas[10] and Shaw and Hipgrave[11] do provide data on the national scene in 1982, three years before our project began. Their surveys showed that at that time, across the British Isles, there were about 50 schemes specifically set up to place teenagers. Most were very small scale with about ten to 20 foster families, each taking one or two difficult teenagers. In 1982, approximately two authorities out of five had special schemes, so our two out of six is only a slightly smaller proportion. Moreover, the two schemes we were able to include were both larger than most so the proportion of specialist foster home placements in our sample was probably a reasonably accurate reflection of the national picture in 1985-7.

During the two years of our survey, County placed 88 adolescents in specialist foster homes and South Thames placed 98. In South Thames, with a large and long-established scheme, all new placements of adolescents were part of the specialist fostering system, whereas County placed selected adolescents in a teen-care scheme which operated alongside more traditional fostering. These differences would make it inappropriate to compare the success of the two schemes, but, in any case, the outcomes were remarkably similar in most respects. Attention will be drawn to any differences when this seems important in understanding the findings, but for the most part, the specialist placements will be considered as one group. It seems best to start with a profile of the 186 new placements and then look at all endings which occurred during the project to see how specialist foster placements turn out. (These 168 endings include some which had started before the project began.) Finally, we make some comparisons between these outcomes and those of teenage placements in 'ordinary' foster homes.

Characteristics
When we looked at all types of fostering, we found that far more teenage girls than teenage boys had placements in foster families. The ratio was 56 per cent girls to 44 per cent boys. In specialist fostering placements the gender split was much more even; 51 per cent girls to 49 per cent boys. The age distribution patterns were also different. Within the 11+ group, it was predominantly the younger ones who were placed in 'ordinary' foster homes but ages of those going to specialist families followed the same curve as all teenage placements with a bulge at age 14–15. (In South Thames, 13 is the minimum age for inclusion in the scheme.) Table 6.8 shows these distributions.

Examination of our data on behaviour problems recorded at the start of the placement shows that adolescents going into specialist placements definitely have more problems than those going into ordinary foster homes. This was particularly marked in South Thames, even though, in this authority, virtually all teenage foster placements are 'specialist'. General unmanageability, school problems, stealing and running away were all noted twice as frequently in specialist placements as in 'ordinary' teenage foster placements.

Table 6.8

Age distribution of foster placements of adolescents

		All	11–13	14–15	16+
Adolescent placements	N =	5694			
of all types	% row	100%	24%	47%	29%
'Ordinary' foster placements	N =	566			
excluding relatives	% row	100%	52%	36%	12%
Relative foster	N =	102			
placements	% row	100%	30%	40%	30%
Specialist foster	N =	186			
placements	% row	100%	19%	54%	27%

The start of the placements

It seems that specialist foster homes are not generally used for teenagers coming into care. Only 59 of the 186 placements (32%) were at admission. It is a great pity that we do not know how long the others had been in care or how many previous placements they had had. We do know that 48 per cent of the specialist placements were moves from residential establishments and 16 per cent were moves from other foster homes. Emergency placements are not quite as prevalent in specialist as in ordinary fostering but nevertheless three in five admission placements and one in five move placements were said to be emergencies. As regards choice, social workers were less likely to code 'only placement available' (12%) and more likely to code 'no choice though seemed OK' (31%) than they were for adolescents going into ordinary foster care where the percentages were 19 per cent and 23 per cent respectively. There was virtually no difference in the other responses. So, in specialist as in other foster placements, social workers reported that there had been other alternatives for about 20 per cent and 'limited choice' for a further 20 per cent.

Several recent research studies have drawn attention to the widespread use of compulsory powers over children in care. Since more teenagers than young children are subject to compulsion and since specialist fostering is particularly concerned with difficult adolescents, we expected to find that rather few of the young people

99

entering specialist foster homes would still be in voluntary care. In fact, we found that half were voluntary cases. There was no difference in this respect between County and South Thames but the latter placed a slightly higher proportion of offenders. In 14 per cent of South Thames placements the young person was on remand or under a criminal or educational care order. The equivalent figure for County was six per cent. There were more cases in County than in South Thames where the authority had assumed parental rights or been given these as a result of Matrimonial or Wardship proceedings.

Aims and expected length

Most specialist foster placements have specific aims and, as Shaw and Hipgrave put it, are 'treatment oriented'. Although there were some placements under each of our aim categories, less than ten per cent were for temporary care and a further 17 per cent for care and upbringing. The largest group (31 per cent overall) came under the aim bridge to independence. Because South Thames has increasingly used specialist homes for most of its adolescent foster placements, aims were more varied in this authority than in County where they were mainly accounted for by treatment (15%), care and upbringing (17%) or bridge to independence (49%).

Table 6.9 compares the primary aims of specialist fostering with those of some other types of placement for adolescents including 'ordinary' fostering.

Obviously, there are close links between a placement's aim and its expected length so it is no surprise to find that only 20 per cent of specialist foster placements were expected to be short-term, i.e. less than eight weeks. Thirty percent were expected to last between eight weeks and a year and 25 per cent between one and two years. More unexpected is the finding that 12 per cent of these placements were planned to last over three years or 'permanently'. (In 13 per cent the expected length was uncertain.) It seems that quite a number of young people going into specialist teenage placements are going to need care for a considerable period.

Endings

It is usually considered one of the special features of specialist fostering that placements should be time limited so 'what happened next?' is an important issue. Our data cannot provide an entirely

Table 6.9

Placement aims for adolescents, by type of placements

	Specialist foster homes	Ordinary foster homes	Lodgings	Children's homes	CHE or young people's centres
N =	186	566	355	1131	714
Temporary care	8%	19%	2%	7%	3%
'Roof'	10%	16%	10%	20%	14%
Remand/punishment	2%	–	2%	5%	28%
Treatment	12%	10%	1%	18%	25%
Assessment	10%	9%	1%	15%	10%
Preparation l.t. foster care	8%	8%	–	8%	1%
Bridge to independence	31%	12%	83%	12%	9%
Care & upbringing	17%	24%	1%	14%	9%
Other	2%	1%	1%	2%	–

satisfactory answer because when the answer to the circumstances of ending question was 'Reached 18 and leaving care' it is not clear whether or not the young person moved out of the placement. Since alternative codings such as 'moved to own flat/bed-sit' were available, the assumption may be that the youngster remained for at least a short while, but we cannot be sure.

Considering that many of those entering specialist homes were already in their mid-teens and that 'bridge to independence' was the most frequent aim, perhaps one would not anticipate that many of these young people would be returning home to live. In fact, almost as many went home from specialist homes (29%) as from 'ordinary' foster homes which had lasted less than two years (33%). But whereas return home from 'ordinary' fostering was usually said to be 'planned', returns from specialist homes were more often 'unplanned'. Returning a young person home may be the last resort if in-care placements have not been able to help.

Twenty-five per cent of specialist placements ended with a move into a residential establishment and 13 per cent to another foster home. In South Thames youngsters tended to go home or to residential care. In County, fewer went home and more moved to new foster homes.

Outcomes
Sustaining specialist foster placements is evidently difficult. Social workers rated only 29 per cent of them as having lasted as long as planned. Ten per cent had lasted longer than planned and in nine per cent of endings there had been no known plan. This leaves more than half the placements (53%) which were said to have ended sooner than planned. That this was not necessarily a bad thing is shown by the fact that rather fewer of them (47%) were said not to have lasted as needed. Nevertheless, this may still be thought a disappointingly high figure of premature endings for a type of placement about which there has been considerable optimism and enthusiasm.

It is important at this point to recall that the aims of most specialist foster placements are among those which are hard to achieve, that adolescents are notoriously difficult creatures with whom to live and for whom to achieve stable in-care placements, and that specialist schemes are set up to deal with young people who have special problems. The next two tables set out the aims, how well they were thought to have been achieved and whether they were considered to have lasted as needed. Both tables show up the difficulties of adolescent placements. The numbers are rather small so percentages can be misleading and it would be unwise to build too much on them. However, treatment and assessment appear to be particularly difficult to achieve for young people going into specialist foster homes. The outcomes of bridge to independence and care and upbringing placements were much more encouraging. Specialist foster placements achieved these aims more often than did 'ordinary' placements for the same age group.

Were the placements helpful?
Further encouragement can be found in the responses to the question on whether the placement was helpful. Of course we only have the

Table 6.10

How far aims were achieved

	All	Temp. care	Roof	Treat-ment	Assess-ment	Prep. l.t. f.c	Bridge	Care & upbring-ing	Other
N =	168	6	18	19	16	7	56	37	9
Fully	15%	50%	50%	10%	–	–	9%	11%	–
In most respects	35%	–	22%	16%	13%	57%	46%	48%	–
Only partially	37%	50%	22%	53%	75%	29%	34%	30%	–
Not at all	13%	–	6%	21%	13%	14%	11%	11%	–

Table 6.11

How placement lasted

	All	Temp. care	Roof	Treat-ment	Assess-ment	Prep. l.t. f.c	Bridge	Care & upbring-ing	Other
N =	168	6	18	19	16	7	56	37	9
As long as needed	42%	100%	56%	42%	19%	29%	46%	32%	44%
Not as long as needed	49%	–	33%	53%	75%	57%	50%	54%	38%
Too long	7%	–	6%	5%	6%	14%	4%	14%	23%
NK	1%	–	6%	–	–	–	–	–	–

103

social workers' views and they may have been over optimistic, but there is no reason to doubt that there were helpful elements even in placements which did not achieve all that was initially hoped for. A third of these foster placements were coded as 'very helpful' and another 40 per cent as 'fairly helpful'. Thus three-quarters were thought to have been beneficial which must surely be considered a satisfactory result for any social work intervention. This rather encouraging finding is reinforced by unpublished studies of special placement schemes carried out by the Social Services Inspectorate in three other authorities. All three reports concluded that the young people were receiving considerable benefit from these foster homes in spite of the difficulties which they brought into these placements.

Fostering by relatives

Only six per cent of all foster starts in our sample were placements with relatives. But this small group of 221 seems worth detailed consideration because of renewed interest in this form of foster care. Three recent studies have given very encouraging reports on the success of relatives as foster parents. Millham[4] found that placements with relatives were considerable more stable than other placements. Berridge and Cleaver[6] also found that placements with relatives were remarkably successful, at least in terms of stability. In our study of long-term foster care[7] we found that foster children brought up by relatives were doing better in virtually every respect than those fostered by non-relatives. It was therefore a considerable surprise and disappointment to discover that relative foster placements in the current project appeared at first sight to be faring no better than the rest. Subsequent analysis showed our relative placements in a much better light. Though they certainly do not match the stability of those in the Berridge and Cleaver report, we suspect that this is linked with differences in the way local authorities use this resource and comparisons may be dangerously misleading.

Age, aim and placement length
We found important age differences between those placed with relatives and the others. At the start of placements, children going to relatives had a rather even age spread. Nearly half (47%) were aged 11 + compared with 16 per cent of those being placed with non-relatives. Only a quarter of the relative placements involve pre-school children

compared with well over half (56%) of the others. When we looked at age at the end of all placements with relatives the picture was the same. We found that 40 per cent were 16 + compared with ten per cent of those with non-relatives and only 13 per cent compared with 48 per cent were pre-school children. Both sets of age difference were clearly linked with differences in placement aim and length of stay. Whereas 40 per cent of non-relative placements were young children needing temporary care during a family emergency, this group accounted for only 18 per cent of relative placements. We also found that although the whole range of placement aims was represented, no less than 50 per cent of all relative placements made during the project were said to be for long-term care and upbringing. By contrast only 11 per cent of unrelated placements had this aim and even fewer were expected to last over three years. Earlier in this chapter, we commented on the number of adolescents being placed for care and upbringing. This finding was even more marked among relative placements where more than half the care and upbringing starts were aged 11 +. Indeed, one in five teenagers being fostered for care and upbringing was going to a relative.

The plan for many of these children and young people was that they remain with their relatives until they could become independent so there were bound to be considerable numbers in the 16 + age group at placement ending. The difference between length of relative and non-relative placements is highlighted by the fact that although relative placements constituted only six per cent of all foster ends, they formed 22 per cent of all placements where the fostering had continued for more than three years.

Clearly, there are major differences in the characteristics of these two types of foster placement. Children going to relatives are on average much older, they are far more likely to be placed with the aim of care and upbringing and their placements are much more often long-stay.

Differences in the way local authorities used relative foster placements
Major differences in the extent to which authorities use this resource have been shown in studies of long-term foster care[7] and of fostering breakdown.[6] They both reported huge differences between authorities in proportions of children fostered by relatives. The six authorities participating in this project do not show such very marked dis-

crepancies though there were variations in usage. In none of them did 'foster home with relatives' account for more than three per cent of new placements of all types, but in some it was only one per cent. However, the length of relative foster placements varied much more dramatically. In Midshire 40 per cent of such placements ended within six months whereas in South Thames only 12 per cent ended that soon. Placements which had lasted more than five years made up 43 per cent of District's relative placement endings compared with 15 per cent in City. It may well be the build-up of long-stay placements in some authorities which contributes to the marked differences in year-end statistics.

Other very noticeable differences between authorities are in the legal status and the aim of relative placements. The proportions of Year 1 placements where the child going to relatives was in voluntary care ranged from less than one in five (South Thames) to four out of five (District), and the proportion on care orders (from care proceedings) went from eight per cent (City) to 67 per cent (South Thames). In all authorities, care and upbringing was the most usual aim, but in Midshire it accounted for only 33 per cent of placements because aims were spread across the range. By contrast, in District all relative placements were for care and upbringing.

Outcomes

As we move on to consider how placements with relatives turn out, it is important to bear in mind the special characteristics of these placements. In the light of their aims and expectations of stay, it is not surprising to find that at the end of relative placements only a third of the children returned to their parents compared with 55 per cent of those leaving unrelated foster homes. For the same reasons, 22 per cent of related fosterings ended when the child reached 18 compared with only four per cent of other foster placements. Proportionately more children and young people left relatives to enter residential establishments (19 per cent compared to 11 per cent), and fewer (14 per cent compared to 24 per cent), moved to other foster homes. Youngsters living with relatives accounted for seven out of a total of 11 moves from foster homes to penal establishments, but for only one out of six moves to a bed and breakfast hotel.

Since rather few relative placements are for the less difficult aim of temporary care, it might be expected that relative placements would score less well overall than others on aims achieved.In fact, the overall scores are very similar. Both types of placement achieved their aim, at least in most respects, in three out of four cases though non-relative placements were more often rated as having achieved the aim 'fully' and in related placements there was an even balance between 'fully' and 'in most respects'.

The same pattern appeared when we looked at whether or not placements lasted as long as needed. Indeed, the figures were almost identical with 66 per cent of both related and non-related placements having lasted as long as required while 23 per cent of the relative foster homes and 24 per cent of the others had ended before the child's needs had been met. It was only on closer analysis that differences, and some explanations for them, began to appear.

The first interesting fact to emerge was that there was considerable variation between authorities as regards relative placements that did not last. In County only 11 per cent of placements with relatives failed to last as needed. In City the proportion that did not last was three times larger at 33 per cent. (This is not accounted for by differences in the proportion of temporary care placements because there were more of these in City than in County.) Since City also makes above average use of relative placements,the outcomes of its placements distort the total picture. Indeed, if City is excluded, the proportion of relative placements which did not last as needed, dips to 17 per cent. The difference between City and County may help to explain the difference in our findings compared with the Berridge and Cleaver study. It may be that their London borough, which made heavy use of relative placements, just happened to be more like our County and less like City.

The second and more important finding was that when each aim was taken separately, we could see that relative placements almost always lasted better, sometimes by only one or two percentage points, sometimes by a larger margin. The only category in which relative placements fared worse was emergency 'roof over head'. Figure 6.2 picks out the 'did not last as needed' category and compares related and unrelated endings under specific aims.(Because we are highlighting the negative in this figure, the lower the percentage, the better the results.)

These figures might seem to contradict our previous statement that there was no overall difference in the success or otherwise of relative

Figure 6.2
Percentage of placements that did not last related to aim

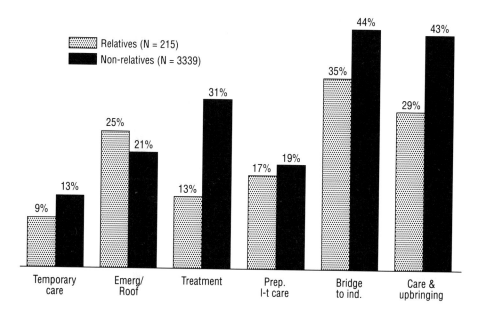

and other foster placements. It may be well to repeat that one in four of the placements in both types of foster home was said not to have lasted as long as needed. The explanation for this apparent contradiction lies in the difference in the proportion of placements with more difficult aims. As we have seen, 40 per cent of endings of non-related foster placements had temporary care for their aim and in temporary care, placement aims are usually met and premature endings are comparatively rare. This bumps up the 'aims achieved' and 'placement lasted' ratings for unrelated foster placements. Relative placements have only half as many temporary care cases, and more of the difficult aims, so they would have to do considerably better to achieve the same average.

When we also bear in mind that children going into related placements were considerably older than those going into other foster homes and that teenagers tend to have far more unsuccessful placements than younger children, the outcomes of placements with relatives begin to look very good. It seems clear that in general, relatives take on older children and often for more complex tasks. They do better with them especially in providing care and upbringing. (Fifty-seven per cent of relative care and upbringing placements were 'successful' compared with 40 per cent with non-relatives.) Social worker ratings on the helpfulness of relative placements are also remarkably high. No less than 50 per cent are rated 'very helpful' and a further 35 per cent 'fairly helpful'.

Organisation, outcomes and the dangers of comparisons
We have to report that we have searched in vain for any clear, consistent and direct links between organisation and placement outcome. This does not mean that organisation has no effect. The presence or absence of specialist staff is evidently a major influence, though not the only influence, on the type of child being placed. The authorities which placed the smallest proportions of teenagers were City, District and North Thames. City had only a handful of fostering specialists in spite of its size. District's fostering unit had not been established long enough to be able to develop a fostering programme for adolescents though the need was recognised. North Thames had no specialist practitioners. By contrast, South Thames with the greatest number of specialist foster care workers, placed the largest proportion of adolescents.

Structures may well affect the quality of service provided but they do not do so in ways that we could measure and, as Chapter 5 has explained, there is no one pattern that can be unreservedly recommended. We found that each system has its own strengths and weaknesses and, of course, it will affect and be affected by the climate, culture, policies and practices of the particular departments in which it operates. The quality of any fostering service will inevitably be strongly affected by the general quality of the department's child care services.

In struggling to understand our data, it has been helpful to have the recent findings of the Berridge and Cleaver research on fostering breakdown. The two authorities they studied had totally different fostering structures, one very specialised, the other not specialised at all. There were striking differences in breakdown rates, too, with the more specialist system at first appearing to be much more successful. Yet careful analysis showed that the differences in breakdown rates were mainly attributable to differences in the characteristics of the children and the type of placement used. They were not due to the differences in the organisation of the service in these two authorities.

Where Berridge and Cleaver found themselves having to explain that what appeared to be the obvious interpretation of different levels of success – namely specialisation and lack of it – was not the real reason, we have the opposite problem. We have to explain that what seems like a considerable and unexpected degree of uniformity in outcome should not be taken at face value.

Throughout this chapter, and earlier in Chapter 3 on patterns of placement, we have noted major differences between the project authorities in their use of foster care, the characteristics of the children they place in foster homes and the aims of their foster placements. It is clear that some authorities make a considerably higher proportion of difficult placements than others. So, looking across the board at a crude rating for 'successful' placements is actually quite misleading because one is not really comparing like with like.

What is needed is a comparative study of placements of children of the same age and background, who have been in foster placements of similar aim and length. Then it might be possible to study the influence of an 'agency' factor in terms of organisation, policy and practice. We cannot do that with our data. In spite of our huge data set, numbers become too low for reliability when foster placements are broken down by authority and by age and by placement aim. Our data also lack sufficient detail and depth, for example, on the children's previous experiences and reactions, and on agency practice.

What we can do is to use our findings to reinforce what we already know, namely that older children are harder to place successfully and that their disturbed, difficult behaviour may be unacceptable to foster parents. We can add to this the clear message that there is a close link between placement aim and placement outcome. From this vantage point, we can see that if a department seeks to increase the proportion of foster family placements for older and disturbed children and tries to use foster home placements to achieve difficult and complex aims, then a somewhat higher breakdown rate must be expected no matter what the skills and dedication of the staff and foster parents.

In the previous section, we recognised that if related foster parents are taking on older children for more difficult aims and are achieving similar success rates to those in 'ordinary' foster homes, they are doing very well. The same principle applies to authorities. If an authority which places a high proportion of teenagers can achieve a success rate somewhere near that of an authority which places mainly young children, its fostering service must be of good quality.

References

1   *Fostering in South Devon: a study of termination of placements 1980–81* Clearing House for Local Authority Social Services Research 6, 28 August 1982.

2   Unpublished report to Avon Social Services Committee, 1982.

3   Packman J with Randall J and Jacques N *Who needs care* Blackwell, 1986.

4   Millham S, Bullock R, Hosie K and Haak M *Lost in care* Gower, 1986.

5   Berridge D *Children's homes* Blackwell, 1985.

6   Berridge D and Cleaver H *Foster home breakdown* Blackwell, 1987.

7   Rowe J, Cain H, Hundleby M and Keane A *Long-term foster care* Batsford Academic/ BAAF, 1984.

8   Keane A 'Behaviour problems' *Adoption & Fostering* 7 3, 1983.

9   Aldgate J and Hawley D 'Fostering disruption' *Adoption & Fostering* 10 2, 1986.

10   Thomas J *Survey of special fostering schemes in London* London Boroughs Regional Planning Committee, 1982.

11   Shaw M and Hipgrave T *Specialist fostering* Batsford Academic/BAAF, 1983.

7 Long-term fostering and adoption

Traditionally, long-term fostering was the heart of the foster care service. Then high breakdown rates disclosed by research studies in the 1960s, and the emphasis on trying to reduce placement moves and secure permanency, led to long-term fostering becoming out of favour with many social workers. In some departments it has become policy to strive for return home or adoption for all young children in long-term care. There is no historical bench mark against which the decline in long-term fostering can be measured but we thought that these placements might have dwindled to a mere trickle. It was not so. We found that long-term fostering is certainly still alive, even if it might not be considered to be very healthy.

Placements
Overall, long-term placements made up nearly ten per cent of all foster placements. This varied from six per cent in South Thames and District to 12 per cent in the two counties. Numerically, long-term foster placements are quite insignificant in relation to the totality of all child care placements, but they remain important because of their immense significance for the individual child. Few children or adolescents being placed for long-term fostering are expected to return home again and even for teenagers a three to five year placement is a long time.

During the two years of the project, our authorities placed 258 children with the expectation that they would remain in their foster families for 'more than five years' or 'permanently'. A further 98 were placed for a stay of three to five years making a total of 356 long-stay placements.

What really surprised us was the large proportion of adolescents – 179 out of the 356 (50%). Whether the number of such placements has gone up or whether it is only an apparent increase due to the shrinking number of young children being placed we cannot say. No doubt the reduction in residential accommodation and the strong emphasis on community care and the benefits of family living will have had some effect, but tradition also seems important. Only ten of the 179 adolescent placements were given the aim of 'bridge to independence' and in only eight was adoption planned. For the rest, social workers selected care and upbringing as the most appropriate of the aims listed on the questionnaire.

It is frustrating that we do not have information about the previous care histories of these young people who, at an age when many of their peers are already looking forward to independence, were needing long-term substitute family care.

Outcomes

As the first chapter explained, the study was designed to provide information about the endings of foster placements that might have been going on for many years and also to monitor the early, crucial months of placements which were made during the project and planned to be long-term.

Taking the historical view first, we find that of the three and a half thousand foster endings included in our survey, about one out of ten (345) had lasted at least three years. Just six per cent (208) had lasted more than five years. Inevitably, the majority of these very long-term cases concerned older teenagers and indeed more than half were aged 16+ at placement ending. Seventy-six of the 345 endings (22%) were relative foster placements. These have had special attention in the previous chapter. Here, all long-term endings are considered together.

Table 7.1 gives the age distribution of these placements and shows the proportions that had lasted as needed and those where the ending was premature even though the fostering had continued for a number of years. It is immediately clear from the table that if a long-term foster placement ends when the child involved is in his or her early to mid-teens, it may well be a premature ending. Long-term foster endings of pre-schoolers are likely to be satisfactory with an unexpected return home or adoption the outcome. If a placement lasts until the young person has reached 16+, a placement is likely to have continued as long as needed. But few foster placements are planned to finish at age 11-15 and these endings frequently spell trouble and a move to another in-care placement. Another point worth noting is that five to 10s are the children whose placements are most likely to be coded as lasting too long.

Table 7.1

How placement lasted, by age at ending

		All	0–4	5–10	11–13	14–15	16+
	N =	345	6	55	53	40	191
Lasted as needed		68%	83%	56%	45%	43%	83%
Did not last as needed		22%	17%	16%	42%	53%	11%
Lasted too long		10%	–	27%	11%	5%	6%
NK		–	–	–	2%	–	–

Of the 345 long-term placement endings, 202 were discharges from care and 143 were moves which include 24 children, mostly teenagers, returning home on trial. The discharges include 56 adoptions, six custodianship orders and a few youngsters moving into independent accommodation but, as one would expect, the most usual discharge endings of long-term foster placements occur when young people graduate out of the child care system at the age of 18. In the previous chapter, reference was made to the overall finding that foster children moved into other foster homes more often than into residential care. In the moves following long-term foster placements, the balance changes. There were 58 moves into residential care compared with 41 moves to other foster homes. However, it is noteworthy that 12 young people aged 16+ moved into a new foster family from a long-term foster placement.

Overall, two-thirds of the long-term foster placements which ended during the project were 'successful' according to our crude measurement of lasting as needed and meeting aims at least in most respects. For the under fives and over 16s this percentage rose sharply to 82 per cent. Social work scores for helpfulness were also high. Only 24 (7%) of the 345 placements which had lasted more than three years were rated as not very helpful or unhelpful. Sixty-nine per cent of those which had lasted more than five years were rated very helpful as were 56 per cent of the three to five year placement endings. It seems therefore that even the placements which did not last as long as needed were quite often felt to have had positive aspects and to have met their aims in most respects. Those that did last were evidently highly regarded.

Only 34 long-term foster endings (10%) fell into our 'unsuccessful' category and in 29 of these the children concerned were aged 11 +. We know that all these placements had continued at least three years but we have no information about their starts and do not know at what age these teenagers had joined their foster families. Nevertheless, our data confirm that adolescence is often a risky time for foster placements. At the beginning of the project we posed the question 'Do many long-term foster homes break down in adolescence?' Sadly, the answer is that quite a lot of them do end prematurely because in addition to the 29 'unsuccessful' endings which would certainly rate as breakdowns, we have seen that another 35 placements did not last as long as needed. Some of these would no doubt be considered breakdowns if more information had been available to us.

The Year 1 placements

Because long-term fostering was of central interest to this study, we looked in great detail at the 194 long-term placements made during the first year of the project and at their status when the project ended. At that point, all of them could have lasted just over a year, while those placed early on could have lasted nearly two years.

By 31 March 1987, 63 of these 194 placements had ended but 11 of these endings proved to be satisfactory outcomes, mostly an unexpected return home or adoption. This leaves 52 endings (27%) which can only be described as breakdowns and two thirds of them involved youngsters aged 11 +. (NB. In the previous part of this chapter we have been looking at the children's age at placement end. Here we are considering age at placement start.)

Table 7.2 shows the steady rise in breakdowns with increasing age at placement and confirms prospectively what we have already seen retrospectively in the previous table. At this stage it is important to point out that the 27 per cent of placements which had already broken down does not constitute the final 'breakdown rate'. All we can say is that within a period of between 13 and 23 months, 27 per cent of the placements had suffered a premature and unsatisfactory ending, but 68 per cent were continuing and five per cent had ended well.

In the Berridge and Cleaver[1] fostering study, 17 per cent of the long-term placements had broken down within the first year. By the end of three years, the proportion had risen to 38 per cent. However, there were major differences between their two authorities with the county's

115

Table 7.2

Status of Year 1 foster placements at project end

		All	0–4	5–10	11–13	14–15	16+
	N =	194	28	60	61	42	3
Satisfactory end		11	2	3	1	4	1
		5%	7%	5%	2%	10%	33%
Continuing		131	25	43	41	22	–
		68%	89%	72%	67%	52%	–
Breakdown		52	1	14	19	16	2
		27%	4%	23%	31%	38%	66%

breakdown rates more than double those in the London borough. They attribute much of this difference to the younger age of the children being placed by the London borough. Since further breakdowns are bound to occur in our sample of long-term placements, it looks as if our final breakdown rate is likely to be very similar to the 38 per cent average for the two authorities in the Berridge and Cleaver study. There were big differences in our authorities, too, with breakdowns ranging from eight per cent to 33 per cent at project end. At first we thought that it would be necessary to echo Berridge and Cleaver's rather depressing conclusion that no great improvement in foster care practice has been achieved since the landmark studies of Parker[2] and George.[3] It was only when we looked at the ages of children at placement in these key research reports that the amazing difference in the populations under study became evident. The comparisons cannot be exact because different researchers have taken slightly different age bands and the periods of follow-up are not identical, but the pattern is so startlingly clear that this does not seem too important.

In Table 7.3 we set out the age at placement for the Parker, George and Berridge studies as well as for our project and Table 7.4 gives the breakdown rates for each age group. (In this table, the 11 'satisfactory ending' cases have been removed from the project sample in order to achieve greater uniformity with the other studies.) Even after taking account of the shorter period of project placements, the improvement in the breakdown rate for young children is quite dramatic.

Considerable improvement has also been achieved in placements of children of primary school age. (Breakdowns by project end were only half the rate reported by Berridge and Cleaver for this age group.) The 37 per cent of breakdowns which have already occurred in the project's teenage placements looks very high. It is higher than in the Berridge study, but George reported a 90 per cent breakdown rate for a small number of adolescents whose placements he studied, although they were not included in his survey because their placements could not have lasted over five years. So there are signs of real progress here, too.

The evidence from the tables below is that while it is true that the breakdown rate in long-term foster placements shows little change, there is an almost complete transformation of the fostering task. Today's social workers are placing adolescents as successfully as their predecessors placed pre-schoolers.

Some comparisons between placements that were continuing and those which had broken down
Detailed examination of the Year 1 placements that had already broken down and comparison with those continuing, reveals the following facts:

• Placements of boys and of girls broke down in equal proportions and in similar age patterns.

• Placements of black and mixed parentage children broke down slightly less often than those of white children. Numbers are small but there is no indication that black children are more at risk at least in the early years of placement.

• More of the children whose placements broke down had come from residential establishments but this is almost certainly because they were older.

• Similarly, 75 per cent of the breakdown children had been in care before compared with 57 per cent of those whose placements were continuing, but this again will be linked with age.

• More than a quarter of the children who suffered a breakdown were receiving remedial education compared with only one in ten of those in continuing placements but physical disability did not have the same

Table 7.3

Comparison of age at placement of children going into long-term foster homes in various studies

	All ages	Pre-school	Primary school age	Secondary school age
Parker 1952–3	N = 108 100%	66%	30%	4%
George 1961–3	N = 112 100%	59%	41%	–
Berridge 1970s	N = 189 100%	51%	42%	6%
Placement outcomes project	N = 194 100%	14%	31%	55%

Table 7.4

Comparison of breakdown rates

% = % breakdown	All ages	Pre-school	Primary school age	Secondary school age
Parker (5 years)	52%	38%	59%	–
George (5 years)	60%	47%	78%	–
Berridge (3 years)	38%	32%	46%	33%
Placement outcomes project (13–23 mos.)	28%	4%	23%	35%

clear associaton with breakdown. Out of ten placements of youngsters with a mild physical disability, three broke down. There were four placements of children suffering moderate or severely disabling conditions. All were continuing at project end.

● Behaviour problems were often reported in cases that broke down. 'Child's behaviour unacceptable to caregivers' was coded as applicable to 33 out of the 52 breakdowns (63%). Interestingly, 'behaviour unacceptable' appeared more often in breakdowns of under 11s than among the teenagers and the child with the highest number of problem behaviours was a four-year-old. In a quarter of the adolescent breakdowns no problem behaviour or only one or two mild problems were recorded. In some of these cases the youngster's behaviour was nevertheless considered unacceptable. While coding errors may occasionally account for this, it seems likely that behaviours not listed on the questionnaire, i.e. insolence or staying out late may have been causing difficulty to foster parents.

The three behaviours where there was the most striking difference between breakdown and continuing cases were 'general unmanage-ability' – present as a serious problem in 23 per cent of breakdown cases and only four per cent of those continuing; 'attention seeking' – a serious problem in 19 per cent of breakdowns and 8% in those continuing; and stealing – a serious problem in 15 per cent of breakdowns but in none of the continuing placements.

● In developing the questionnaires we felt it appropriate to ask for information about children's positive qualities as well as their behaviour problems. We also wondered if it would be possible to discover whether the presence of qualities such as being cheerful, responsive and affectionate might enable foster parents to tolerate problem behaviour. In the event, we were worried about subjectivity and somewhat doubtful about the validity of some responses and the task of linking qualities with behaviour and outcomes would have been too complex and time consuming for us to accomplish. However, we did find noticeable differences in the ratings on positive qualities in the breakdown and continuing groups. These differences proved to be statistically significant*, so although we would not want to make them appear more 'scientific' than they really are, the topic seems sufficiently interesting to make it worth setting out a few findings in Figure 7.1. It is also worth mentioning that in 50 per cent of the breakdown cases, social workers did not code the child or adolescent concerned as 'definitely' having any of the six qualities listed. This compares with 31 per cent in the continuing group.

---

* 'definitely responsive to adults', $x^2 = 4.71$, df = 1, p $<$ .05
'definitely affectionate to adults', $x^2 = 5.42$, df = 1, p $<$ .05
'definitely cheerful disposition', $x^2 = 7.37$, df = 1, p $<$ .01

Figure 7.1
Differences in positive qualities

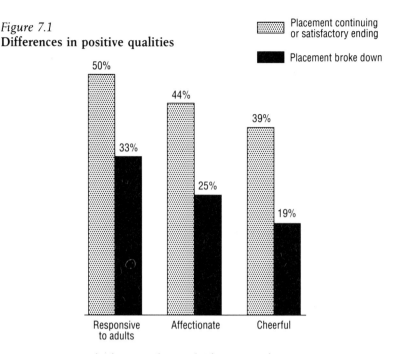

Comparisons with the Berridge and Cleaver study
Berridge and Cleaver found that in addition to age there were various factors associated with placements that lasted or broke down. Although our broader, more superficial survey did not cover all the topics examined in the Berridge study, we hoped that our sample would show similar patterns and thus support useful indicators for good practice. Unfortunately, our findings do not offer clear support though they are not necessarily contradictory.

Berridge and Cleaver found that children who remained in care on a voluntary basis had significantly fewer breakdowns than those committed by courts. Our cases do not show a consistent pattern and there are no statistically significant differences.

Separation from siblings who are also in care was found to be associated with placement breakdown in the Berridge study. Our retrospective data on all long-term foster ends showed the opposite. Fewer children whose placement outcomes were 'unsuccessful' had been separated from siblings who were also in care. It may be that much more detail is needed before proper comparisons can be made.

For example, some children experience distressing separation from siblings they feel close to, while others are only technically separated from siblings they have never met.

The effect of family contact – or lack of it – on fostering outcomes is always difficult to measure because so many factors interact. What we can report with confidence is that in six per cent of the 345 long-term endings contact had not been allowed and in another 30 per cent none had occurred. Nearly one child in four (23%) had been having contact with his or her family at least monthly but the largest group (40%) was made up of children who had infrequent contact, i.e. only quarterly or occasionally.

Berridge and Cleaver report: 'some indication of an inverse relationship between the degree of parental contact and levels of breakdown. However, the differences are insufficient to be statistically significant.' Our findings are also inconclusive. If we compare our 'successful' and 'unsuccessful' groups (excluding children placed with relatives), we find that nearly a quarter of the 'successful' (23%) had had weekly or monthly contact compared with 15 per cent of the 'unsuccessful'. But when we look at the proportions with no contact at all, we find that the balance swings the other way. More of the successful had had no contact (39%-30%). It looks from this as if occasional contact may create more difficulties than either frequent contact or none. However, this conjecture is not supported by the findings on parental contact in the Year 1 placements. Of the 44 placements with non-relatives which had already broken down, 14 had had no family contact, 15 had had infrequent contact and 15 had had contact at least monthly and often weekly. (We cannot compare the breakdowns with the 'continuing' cases because our data on contact come from the end of placement questionnaires and, of course, in continuing placements these were not completed.)

On one factor at least there was clear agreement between the findings of the two studies. In both, experienced foster parents were markedly more successful. Berridge and Cleaver report four times as many breakdowns when foster parents had less than a year's experience. Our findings are much less dramatic but point in the same direction. Half the foster parents in our breakdown group had been approved less than a year previously compared with 38 per cent in the continuing group. (Relative foster parents were excluded, since virtually all of them are approved just in relation to the placement).

121

Concluding findings about the Year 1 breakdown cases
Nearly a quarter of the placements (23%) had lasted over a year before they broke down, 38 per cent ended between seven and 12 months after placement, 25 per cent lasted between two and six months, and 13 per cent less than two months.

Only three of the 52 children returned home but another went to friends. One, fostered by his grandmother, went into custody and two young siblings went to prospective adopters. Seventeen youngsters (33%) went to other foster families usually with the aim of being prepared for another long-term placement. But much the largest group (54%) went into residential care.

Foster home breakdowns are an event which most social workers dread. They are bound to be deeply distressing to children and foster parents too, especially when the placement was intended to be long term. Our question about helpfulness is much too simplistic to deal adequately with a situation of such complexity and social workers may have been unwilling to face the pain for the child. However, it may be reassuring to note that 60 per cent of these breakdown endings were coded as having been at least fairly helpful.

Adoption and custodianship
We started the chapter on foster care by saying how different the reality is from what one might expect from reading the professional literature. It was the same with our adoption findings only more so. Infant adoptions were surprisingly numerous, adoption placements of older or handicapped children were fewer than we had expected and only six custodianship orders were made during the two years of the project.

In reporting the adoption work of our six authorities, we need to include both placements with adoptive families and placements with foster parents where the aim is that they should adopt the child. The two kinds of placement cannot be satisfactorily disentangled because some authorities take into care infants to be placed for adoption. Their new families may be technically foster parents for the first few weeks or months. Other infants are not admitted to care but placed under the Adoption Agencies Regulations. A further complication is that some foster placements with the aim of adoption are really adoptive placements right from the start, whereas others are long-term fostering with the hope that adoption will ultimately prove possible.

Our data do not permit us to distinguish between these explicit and implicit aims. For the sake of clarity in this section, we bring together both adoptive placements and foster placements where the aim is adoption, distinguishing them only when this seems necessary.

We found major differences in the amount and type of adoption work being done by project authorities. The number of adoption placements may not be in proportion to other child care work. Thus County, which made only 17 per cent of all the placements included in the project, made 34% of the adoption placements, while the two London boroughs which between them made 20 per cent of all placements, account for only ten per cent of the adoptions. It also seems as though the presence of a central unit dealing with the adoption of babies may have the effect of inhibiting consideration of adoption for older children for, as Table 7.5 shows, City and Midshire place very few of them. It is quite remarkable that only six out of City's 2663 placements of school age children had the aim 'adoption by this family'.

Over the two years of the project, the six authorities between them made 261 placements where the aim was adoption. Of these, only 40 were children over five years old and 19 of these were County's cases. When we looked closely at the 221 pre-school placements, we found that the great majority (182) were young infants. There were eight older infants aged one but not yet two, 18 two-year-olds, five aged three and eight aged four.

Table 7.5

Number of placements where the aim is adoption

		All	City	District	Mid-shire	County	North Thames	South Thames
	N =	261	74	29	42	89	14	13
0–4	N =	221	68	24	41	70	10	8
5–10	N =	32	5	5	–	14	4	4
11–13	N =	6	1	–	1	4	–	–
14–15	N =	2	–	–	–	1	–	1

Of the 221 pre-school adoption placements, 191 involved white children and 30 black (three Afro-Caribbean, two Asian, one 'other' and 24 mixed parentage). Eight of the 32 placements of five to ten-year-olds involved black children – all of them were of mixed parentage. There were no black children among the teenage adoption placements.

Handicapped or disabled children do not feature greatly in these adoptions. Of course many were very young, but out of the 261 placements, there were only 17 children (7%) who had a diagnosed moderate or severe intellectual impairment or were pre-schoolers expected to need special educational provision. Nine of these 17 also had a moderate or severe physical disability. There were no children with a serious physical disability but no mental impairment. In addition, six of the children being placed were receiving remedial education and there were 11 others with mild physical problems but average intelligence.

Outcomes

Since there might be little time for problems to emerge in placements made in the second year of the project, we need to confine consideration of outcome to the 126 placements which were made in Year 1. Almost all the 105 placements of under fives appear to have gone smoothly. Two infants were withdrawn by their natural parents and there were two breakdowns in the under five age group. One of these involved an infant (reasons for breakdown unclear to us) and one involved a four-year-old with a moderately severe intellectual handicap and many serious behaviour problems.

During Year 1 there were 18 placements of children aged five to ten and three of youngsters aged 11+. Nine of these 21 placements were into adoptive homes and 12 were fostering with the aim of adoption. Table 7.6 shows the type of placement, the age distribution and the number of breakdowns that had occurred by the end of the project.

Taking both types of placement together, we can see that in all, seven placements or one in three had broken down during a period of 13-23 months. These figures may be a cause of some dismay and it is important to set them in context. The first point to remember is that the numbers are small and we are only talking about one year. It is also noteworthy that of these seven children, two siblings and one other child had already had a breakdown in an adoptive or long-term foster

Table 7.6

Placements and breakdowns of school age children

		Placed in an adoptive home		Fostered – aim adoption	
		Placed	Broke down	Placed	Broke down
5 –10	N = 18	9	(1)	9	(4)
11+	N = 3	–	–	3	(2)
Total placed	21	9	(1)	12	(6)
Total breakdowns	7				

home and another child was a 15-year-old with a severe intellectual handicap.

Since County is the most active in seeking adoption for older children, most of the breakdowns come from County. But lest anyone conclude that County's practice is at fault, we must hasten to say that County does not have a particularly high proportion of long-term fostering breakdowns.

The most useful comparative figures come from a current study by Thoburn and Rowe[4] of over a thousand 'permanent' placements made by voluntary societies between 1980 and 1984. Preliminary figures show a 28 per cent disruption rate for placements of school age children within 18 months to five years of placement. There is a steep rise toward the teen years. The Thoburn and Rowe study also shows that placements of disabled children are less vulnerable to breakdown than are placements of those who have behavioural or emotional problems.

Our project numbers are too small and our knowledge of the cases too limited for us to make any sensible comment about whether fostering with a view to adoption is a more hazardous route than direct adoption placement. The difference in the proportion of disruptions may be just chance or the children placed for fostering may be older (at the top end of each age band), or have more serious problems. Perhaps all one can say is that fostering first does not seem to be advantageous.

There are some other interesting points about these seven adoption breakdowns. First, all of them involved white children. Second, all except the baby had been in care on at least one previous occasion. Thirdly, in six out of the eight cases the child's behaviour was said to be unacceptable to the new parents. Most of them did have a variety of reported behaviour problems but there did not seem to be any particular pattern in these. Only three of the seven (including the baby) scored 'definitely' on any of the positive qualities listed on the questionnaire. As we saw in the chapter on foster care, absence of positive qualities may have some association with placement breakdown.

Adoption by long-term foster parents
One other aspect of adoption work calls for report and comment and that is adoption by long-term foster parents.

Out of 345 endings of foster placements which had lasted three years or more, we found 62 endings through adoption. This is 18 per cent. Well over half of these had in fact lasted for more than five years. In 27 of these 62 long-term foster parent adoptions, the child concerned was already a teenager though only six cases were of 16 year olds being adopted on the brink of independence.

Custodianship
Custodianship hardly figures in our findings. Over the two years, there were just six custodianship orders made. Five of these were in County and one in City. Four concerned children fostered by relatives. These are of course just the sort of cases that custodianship was intended to assist. In five cases the children were in the under 11 age group and the sixth was aged 12.

References

1 Berridge D and Cleaver H *Foster home breakdown* Blackwell, 1987.

2 Parker R *Decision in child care: a study of prediction in fostering* Allen & Unwin, 1966.

3 George V *Foster care* RKP, 1970.

4 Thoburn J and Rowe J 'A snapshot of permanent substitute family placement' *Adoption & Fostering* 12 3, 1988.

8 Residential care

It is more than a decade since the publication of Prosser's *Perspectives on residential child care*[1] which drew attention to 'the dearth of evidence concerning different types of residential care and the effects of different types of care on different types of children'. Since that time, the residential scene has changed a great deal, but the dearth of evidence continues. The paucity of research on residential services is really quite extraordinary considering the large number of children and young people who experience these services and the high cost of providing them.

It is certainly no accident that the best researched type of residential care is the most expensive, namely observation and assessment centres. However, as Fuller's[2] monograph on issues in assessment makes clear, much still remains to be learned about how these resources are used let alone how effective they are when compared with other methods of assessing children's needs and capacities.

Drastic reductions in the number of places in Community Homes with Education and the metamorphosis of some CHEs into Young People's Centres appear to have been effected with a minimum of research from a child care perspective; though when it comes to CHEs, study of delinquency overlaps with study of other aspects of child care. Research into delinquency has inevitably focused on outcomes and effectiveness, so more attention has been paid to regimes and outcomes in CHEs than to the regimes and outcomes of other child care establishments.

A major difficulty has been the inevitable time lag in research on the long-term effect of residential care. Thus, important studies such as Tizard,[3] Triseliotis and Russell,[4] and Rutter, Quinton and Liddle[5] describe institutions such as residential nurseries and cottage homes which now virtually do not exist.

Until the appearance of Berridge's[6] study *Children's homes* in 1985, there was virtually no up-to-date research or, indeed, any information on how Children's Homes were being used. Berridge's findings were supported and strengthened by an extensive study of community homes for children which was carried out by the Social Services Inspectorate of the DHSS[7] in 1985. These two publications provide a wealth of descriptive material and include evaluations of the homes' purposes, regimes and standards. However, neither Berridge nor the Social Services Inspectors set out to examine outcomes or to make systematic comparisons between placements in Children's Homes and other types of residential care or between the outcomes of residential care and foster family care.

Although our data on residential care is less detailed and in some respects much less satisfactory than our data on foster care, it is important in its own right. In a modest and limited way it can help to fill a few gaps and answer some questions and, of course, the comparison with foster care remains important.

The changing scene
The dilemmas and uncertainties surrounding residential care and the basic prejudices against it have been helpfully outlined by Davis.[8] These difficulties and disappointments, allied to anxieties about high costs, came together as a major force for change in the mid-70s. The result was that when fieldwork for this project started in April 1985, residential services were emerging from a period of upheaval and changing focus. Many local authorities had cut their provision drastically and a few such as Warwickshire actually closed all their children's establishments.

In its report on children in care published the previous year,[9] the House of Commons Select Committee had said that these changes 'may be optimistically typed as being a process of transition, but less optimistically viewed, sometimes look like a gradual process of destruction.' Residential care had been under fire both from those who saw it as an ineffective response to delinquency and urged the development of Intermediate Treatment and community projects, and from those who saw it as an inappropriate milieu in which to bring up children. Many CHEs and Children's Homes had been closed and for others radical changes in style and purpose were planned or already in process. Our six authorities had experienced every level of change from minimal to an almost complete transformation. Changes and developments continued throughout the project so we found ourselves trying to describe a constantly moving picture.

Even without all the recent developments, the residential scene would be difficult to write about because of its complexity and variety. The first problem is that the term 'residential care' includes many different types of establishment. These range from family group homes (which may closely approximate a large foster home), to secure accommodation in a closed setting; from therapeutic centres to some very authoritarian CHEs; from family centres, evolving from residential or day nurseries, to young people's centres which combine the functions of an observation and assessment centre and a CHE. (Hostels are not included in our residential category, but some information about hostel placements can be found in Chapter 9.)

The second difficulty is that one finds the same name given to establishments which have almost nothing in common and different names given to facilities which appear to be very much the same. Thus we found an observation and assessment centre in City that could take up to 100 young people in a number of separate units while down in North Thames, observation and assessment was carried out in a very small, informal unit which was closely linked with a non-residential service run by the Education Welfare Service for truants and children with other school problems.

In our questionnaires, we used the title Children's Home instead of the more technically correct Community Home because we wanted to distinguish different types of community home. 'Children's Home' still covered a huge variety of establishments. At one end of the spectrum were small, long-stay family style units for quite young children, often those with some form of disability or handicap. At the other extreme were homes with 30 or more beds for difficult adolescents or large, multi-function establishments for all ages and varying lengths of stay.

Our resources did not enable us to make a coherent visiting plan but we saw a number of establishments during our fieldwork and at meetings with social workers for planning or report-back sessions. The differences we both saw and heard about are so great that it almost seems inappropriate to speak of residential child care as though it were an entity.

The project findings
Instead of the 'process of destruction' feared by the Select Committee and others, our data disclose continued heavy reliance on the

residential sector. In spite of the considerable reduction in places during recent years, it clearly continues to play a major role in child care services. Residential establishments of one kind or another provided a third (36%) of all the placements made during the project and half (52%) of the placements of adolescents. Two out of five children and young people admitted to care during the project had their first placement in a residential establishment. (This is a lower proportion than in the Dartington study where just over half of all admission placements were in residential care.)

Once again, we were struck by the large number of placements. The static picture provided by annual returns gives no idea of the turnover. Young people flow in and out of residential establishments with remarkable rapidity. In the course of the first year of the project, the six authorities provided 1859 residential placements and by the end of the second year, 93 per cent of these placements had ended and the beds were no doubt filled up again. The workload involved must be very heavy for fieldworkers, residential staff and administrators.

In Chapter 3 of this report we drew attention to very considerable differences in the proportion of residential placements made by our project authorities. Figure 8.1 below shows the way in which our authorities used residential care for different age groups. It also highlights the major part played by the residential sector in providing about half of the placements for adolescents in all the authorities. It is difficult to determine how much the use of residential placements depends on availability, but it seems likely that if beds are easily available they tend to get used.

Some readers may be surprised by the percentages of pre-school and primary school age children having residential placements. For children aged under 11, about one placement in four was in a residential establishment – almost always a Children's Home. The proportion rises to 46 per cent in District and sinks to 11 per cent in Midshire. Far fewer pre-schoolers had a residential placement and this category includes hospital placements for newborns or children on place of safety orders. Staff in City reported increased use of Children's Homes for young children who had been sexually abused.

There were also some particular reasons why more pre-schoolers had residential placements in District, and in North and South Thames. In District, the absence of a night duty team meant that young children might be taken to a Children's Home by the police or other

Figure 8.1
Per cent of residential placements, by age and authority

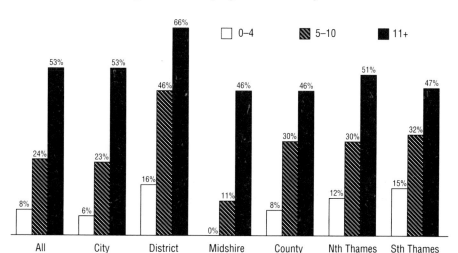

emergency services. Their stay was usually short. In North Thames, the emphasis on relief care and the use of local community services also led to residential placements for some young children. In South Thames, pre-school residential placements were mainly in locally based Family Centres which may care for very young children. They were usually either with their mothers or in family groups.

In addition to variation in overall use of residential care, we found very big differences in the type of establishments in which authorities place their children. In City, getting on for half (46%) of all residential placements were in observation and assessment centres, whereas in County, 75 per cent of residential placements were in Children's Homes and only two per cent in observation and assessment centres. Midshire made heavy use of its Young People's Centres (44%) while CHE/YPCs made up only three per cent of residential placements in North Thames. This diversity of policy and practice is still further emphasised by recollection of our earlier comments on the major differences in size and style of establishments in the same category.

A further complication to analysis and comparison arises from our findings on the overlapping functions of the various types of establishment. When we looked at the aims of placements it became clear that observation and assessment centres are not just used for assessment, that CHEs and YPCs may provide for young people needing care and upbringing and that the aims of Children's Home placements for adolescents spread across all the possibilities provided for in our questionnaires.

Table 8.1

Placement aim, by type of establishment in Year 1 (children aged 11+)

	Children's home	O & A centre	CHE/YPC
N =	591	486	359
Temporary care	8%	4%	3%
Emergency/roof	18%	19%	14%
Treatment	19%	11%	28%
Assessment	14%	32%	9%
Preparation long-term placement	10%	–	3%
Care & upbringing	14%	1%	10%
Bridge to independence	12%	2%	9%
Remand	4%	28%	22%
Other/NK	2%	2%	3%

Placements in family centres, secure units and 'other' residential establishments are excluded from this table.

Social workers' attitudes to residential care seem to be rather ambivalent and affected by their authority's policy and resources. As noted in earlier chapters, residential care is much more likely than foster care to be considered inappropriate. One in five Children's Homes and observation and assessment placements was coded 'doubtful' or 'unsuitable' as were one in four of the CHE/YPC placements. (This compares with six per cent 'doubtful' or 'unsuitable' ratings for foster placements.) It was noteworthy that social workers in

City and District where residential care was plentiful and much used, most often considered the placements appropriate, while in Midshire, with the lowest percentage of residential placements, social workers were more likely to be critical. Indeed, nearly half (48%) of Midshire's CHE/YPC placements were coded as 'doubtful' or 'inappropriate' compared with an average of 24 per cent for the six authorities. Whether Midshire's workers were dissatisfied with the limited range of placements available, or were reflecting an anti-residential feeling in this authority, our data cannot reveal.

The residents
In his book on Children's Homes, David Berridge pointed out that this name was no longer very appropriate since these days most of their beds are filled with adolescents. Our data amply confirm this. Three quarters (78%) of all Year 1 Children's Home placements were of young people aged 11+. Pre-schoolers accounted for just six per cent and the under 11s for 16 per cent.We also found that younger children generally stay for shorter periods so that at any one time, the great majority of Children's Home residents will be adolescents. Very few children under the age of eleven are admitted to observation and assessment centres and virtually none to CHEs or YPCs, so local authority residential provision is essentially a service for adolescents.

For reasons that, as far as we know, have never been clarified, there are always more boys than girls admitted to care. In this project the overall ratio of male to female admissions is 56 per cent to 44 per cent. For adolescent admissions it is 57 per cent to 43 per cent. Since more boys are admitted as offenders and since offenders have more changes of placement, it is not surprising to find that 61 per cent of teenage placements involve boys. However, boys are not equally spread across all types of placement and within the residential sector they feature more prominently in CHEs (75%) and less prominently in Children's Homes (52%). Boys make up 62 per cent of teenagers entering observation and assessment centres but 71 per cent of placements in secure units.

One of the often cited advantages of residential care over foster homes is its capacity to provide for groups of siblings without having to split them up. Our findings do not provide any strong support for this claim. If we look first at the under 11s, our data show that in 60 per cent of residential placements the child was with at least one sibling. This

133

compares with 54 per cent of foster home placements for this age group so there is not a large difference, but the opportunity to remain with siblings probably accounts for the choice of a residential placement for at least some of this age group. Of course children may be placed on their own because their siblings are not in care or they may have no siblings. If we examine the figures closely, we find that in 14 per cent of residential placements of the under 11s the child was placed alone but had one or more siblings in another in-care placement. The figure for foster placements is virtually identical at 15 per cent.

Adolescents rather seldom have residential placements with a sibling. We found that in only 273 out of the 3309 residential placement endings of the over 11s had the young person concerned been placed with a sibling (8%). Two-thirds of those young people who had one or more siblings in care were separated from them, but in the majority of cases, siblings were not in care. Fewer foster home endings for this age group reported siblings in care but separated from the study child, but at 50 per cent, the proportion separated still seems very high. The comparison is not very satisfactory, however, because these foster home endings included some long established placements whereas most residential placements had been relatively short. It seems that neither foster care nor residential care is particularly successful in keeping family groups together (or bringing them together if they enter care separately). We can echo the Social Services Inspectorate's comment in its 1985 report[5] on community homes: 'There was little evidence that the homes were being used to keep families together. The extent of sibling separation was of some concern and may merit closer study...'

Our data on family contact are quite limited but we found that half (51%) of the children and young people leaving residential placements had been in touch with their families at least once a week. Only 14 per cent had had no family contact and some of these placements would have been very short.

Another argument for the need to maintain a strong residential sector is the greater capacity of residential establishments to cope with difficult behaviour and our findings offer some support for this. As we studied the social workers' reports of serious behaviour problems at placement starts, we found that residential establishments do indeed accept the more difficult youngsters. Observation and assessment centres and CHEs are, of course, specifically intended to deal with difficult young people. Specialist foster homes are also set up to help youngsters with problems, so the most relevant comparison is between Children's Homes and 'ordinary' foster homes.

We found that many problems were between two and three times more likely to be reported as 'serious' for children and young people going into Children's Homes than into 'ordinary' foster homes. This difference appeared in all age groups, but inevitably, adolescents have a wider range of problem behaviours. Some examples of the comparative incidence of these problems in the 11+ age group include: 'general unmanageability', foster home placements eight per cent, Children's Homes 18 per cent; stealing five per cent and 13 per cent; truancy five per cent and 18 per cent; running away five per cent and 15 per cent.

Some problem behaviours do not show up so much more often in residential placements. Thus attention-seeking was said to be 'serious' in 12 per cent of teenage foster placements and 15 per cent of teenage Children's Home placements and the incidence of inappropriate sexual behaviour was six per cent and nine per cent.

Comparison of placements in Children's Homes, observation and assessment centres and CHEs shows a somewhat lower proportion of problem behaviour in young people being admitted to Children's Homes. The largest difference is in the incidence of stealing. This was said to be a serious problem for 13 per cent of adolescents going into Children's Homes and for 27 per cent and 32 per cent of those entering observation and assessment centres or CHEs/YPCs. For 'general unmanageability' the proportions are 18 per cent, 24 per cent and 27 per cent; for truancy, 18 per cent, 27 per cent and 25 per cent and for running away 15 per cent, 29 per cent and 27 per cent.

For a variety of reasons it has not been possible for us to achieve a fully satisfactory analysis of the behaviour of children and young people in residential care and its possible effect on outcome. We can report that whereas the child's behaviour was said to be unacceptable to caregivers in only three per cent of residential placement endings of children under 11 years old, this rose to 16 per cent for endings of adolescent placements. However, residential establishments definitely do seem able to cope with a higher level of problem behaviour than is tolerable even in specialist foster families. This emerges from our finding that the young person's behaviour was said to be unacceptable in 32 per cent of specialist foster placement endings and 29 per cent of teenage endings in unrelated foster placements (nearly twice the rate for residential establishments which was 16 per cent). For methodological reasons explained earlier, we cannot always separate types of residential establishment at ending, but the indications are that as one might expect, problem behaviour is somewhat less acceptable to staff in Children's Homes than in CHEs or observation and assessment centres. The problems most frequently linked with the coding 'unacceptable' are aggression, general unmanageability and running away. If we had the caregivers' views, the picture might have been different.

Placement length and endings
Most residential placements are short. Of the 3763 that ended during the project, nearly a third (31%) had lasted less than a month and only four per cent had gone on for more than three years. Younger children's placements end sooner than the placements of teenagers which are more evenly spread between a week and one to two years. There is a general similarity across the authorities with the single exception that, as with other types of placement, County has more residential placements that last a long time.

In about a fifth of all residential placements no plan was made about expected length. After taking this into account, we find that nearly half (47%) last as long as planned, nearly a third (31%) do not last as planned but one in five (21%) lasts longer. A shorter stay than planned may not mean an unsatisfactory outcome. Well over half (59%) of all residential placements lasted as long as the children needed them, 21 per cent did not last and 17 per cent were felt to have gone on too long. It therefore looks as if lasting longer than planned was usually because other plans could not be accomplished rather than because the child needed a longer than expected stay. There are no major differences between our authorities in this respect.

Next to 'return' home which accounted for 41 per cent of residential endings, the most usual way for placements to end was with a move to another residential establishment. There were over a thousand such moves during the project and they account for 29 per cent of all residential endings. A further eight per cent of placements were moves into lodgings, a flat or bed-sit and six per cent went to penal establishments. It is interesting that the flow of children going in and out from residential to foster care and vice versa is almost in balance. There were 379 children who left residential establishments for foster homes (70 per cent of these were aged +) and 398 youngsters came into residential care following a foster placement (71 per cent of these were also aged 11 +). No doubt some of these moves concerned the same children but we have not been able to trace the placement patterns of individuals.

In view of the talk about closures, it may be of interest to note that over the two year period there were 115 residential endings associated with closures. They were spread across all authorities in roughly the proportions one would expect from the size of the in-care populations.

Placements in secure units
There were 102 secure unit placements reported during the project. This is probably an undercount because some of the larger establishments had secure accommodation within them and young people may well have moved in and out without change of placement notifications being completed. Of these 102 placements, 24 were as admissions and 78 were in-care moves. They represent between one per cent and four per cent of all teenage placements in the six authorities. Some youngsters had several secure accommodation placements for the 102 placements involved only 76 young people.

Although there were only eight placements where the young person was still in voluntary care, one admission in four was a young person not on 'offender' status. Exactly three out of four were boys.

Outcomes
Using the project's crude measure of 'successful' and 'unsuccessful' we find that 46 per cent of all residential endings rate as successful and 16 per cent unsuccessful. The least 'successful' were where placements ended when young people were aged 11-15.

Once again we find that 'success' or lack of it is closely related to the aim of placement and differences are statistically significant.* Thus 71 per cent of all residential placement ends rated as 'successful' when the aim had been temporary care. This hopeful percentage drops to 48 per cent of placements with the aim of assessment, 37 per cent where the aim was bridge to independence and a low of 34 per cent for placements aiming for treatment.

In spite of all the differences in the way residential care was used in

---

*$df = 9$, $x^2 = 79.49$, $p < .001$

the six authorities, there is a quite remarkable apparent similarity in their 'success' rates with a range of only seven per cent. The London boroughs had the lowest rate of 'successful' endings (North Thames 42 per cent and South Thames 43 per cent). The two counties did marginally better (Midshire 46 per cent, County 45 per cent), and City and District's much used residential services did best (City 48 per cent, District 49 per cent). If the under 11s are excluded, the percentage of 'successful' endings drops slightly and the pattern changes slightly. Now City, District and Midshire have a higher proportion of 'successful' placements than County, North Thames and South Thames but the differences are still too small to be statistically significant.

In considering this phenomenon, it is essential to keep in mind the limitations on our measure of 'success'. It is not a measure of the quality of service and its deficiencies are highlighted when it is being used in relation to the wide variety of establishments that together make up residential care. Nevertheless, the finding that in no authority did even half the residential placements both last as needed and meet their aims, does serve to point up the difficulty of maintaining placements and achieving goals no matter what the setting may be.

Within residential care's overall 'success' rate of 46 per cent, it is interesting to make some comparisons between different types of establishment. Observation and assessment centres come out best with 52 per cent of placements having lasted as needed and met their aims at least in most respects. Children's Homes follow with 40 per cent 'successful' and CHEs/YPCs have the least satisfactory score of 36 per cent. This pattern holds good quite consistently. Whether the aim of the placement is temporary care, treatment, assessment or bridge to independence the observation and assessment centre placements were said to have achieved the aim more often than placements in Children's Homes. Placements in CHEs and YPCs were not only least likely to achieve the stated aim, but also least likely to last as needed.

In view of recent criticisms of observation and assessment centres, it may seem quite surprising that they should apparently be achieving better results than Children's Homes, especially as they take in more of the older adolescents. However, Millham and colleagues[10] had somewhat similar findings in their cohort study. They found that observation and assessment placements broke down less often than placements in Children's Homes or CHEs. A much more detailed study is needed before really valid comparisons could be made, but it has been suggested to us that expectations of what can be achieved in observation and assessment centres are both more restricted and more realistic, especially in relation to remands. Observation and assessment centres also tend to be better staffed than Children's Homes. It is also worth considering whether they provide a clearer structure and a sharper focus which assists in achieving aims and maintaining placements.

When it comes to ratings on helpfulness the pattern changes somewhat. Sixty-seven per cent of Children's Home placements were rated by social workers as having been very helpful (21%) or fairly helpful (46%). Observation and assessment centres scored slightly lower with 63 per cent and CHEs again rank bottom with only 56 per cent placements rated very or fairly helpful. Our data on helpfulness are, of course, very 'soft' and social workers might code placements as helpful for the wrong reasons. Nevertheless, within their limitations, the comparisons are interesting.

When we look at the overall ratings on helpfulness of residential placements, four of the six authorities can be seen to have very similar results, but Midshire and County stand out as different. In Midshire social workers took a relatively jaundiced view of the helpfulness of residential placements and rated 30 per cent as 'not very helpful' or 'unhelpful'. County social workers were just the opposite. Only 13 per cent of their residential placements received these pessimistic helpfulness ratings. Since Midshire's 'success' rates were at least average, and County's 'success' rate for adolescents was below average, these differing perceptions cannot be explained by our data on outcomes but they do tie in with our finding that Midshire social workers rather more often coded residential placements as 'doubtful' or 'unsuitable'.

Residential care or foster care?
Our findings will not offer much ammunition to either side in the continuing debate about how far the residential sector should be reduced and greater reliance placed on foster family care. There are no clear cut answers to be found in a comparison of our outcomes data on residential and foster placements. Indeed, the 'success' rates are almost identical. The inevitably superficial instruments of a large scale

survey cannot measure the psychological benefits or damage that result from these placements. What we can do is to provide some facts that can help to curb some of the more extreme claims and allegations.

Nowadays, pre-school children are almost never placed in residential care except for very special reasons and there is no evidence to suggest that this pattern should be changed. However, because large numbers of pre-schoolers go into foster homes and their placements tend to be more successful than those of older children, this skews overall outcome patterns. So, when comparing foster family and residential care, it seems best to exclude the under fives and focus on the under 11s and the adolescents.

There is no doubt that foster homes more often suffer premature endings in that they are said not to have lasted as long as the children needed them. Looking at all placement endings which occurred during the study, we find that 20 per cent of foster placements which ended when the child was aged five to 10 had failed to last as long as needed. This compares with 13 per cent of residential endings. For endings where the child was aged 11+, the percentage of premature endings is 38 per cent for foster home and 22 per cent residential placements.

When it comes to the other crucial issue of whether the placement aims were met, the pattern changes. There is little difference here between the two types of care. In three out of four (76%) foster placements of the five to 10s the aims were met fully or in most respects. Residential placements for this age group were marginally better at meeting aims with 78 per cent scoring fully or in most respects. For adolescents, the foster home placements were slightly more likely to have met their aims – 63 per cent met at least in most respects compared with 60 per cent of residential endings.

The effect of bringing together the answers to questions on lasting and meeting aims into our project definition of 'success' is to wipe out the difference between foster and residential endings. Presumably this is because if a foster home lasts it usually achieves its aim, too, whereas in residential care there may more often be a mis-match between lasting and achieving objectives. Neither type of placement can claim to be very successful in dealing with adolescents.

As far as social workers' judgements on the helpfulness of the placement are concerned, we find that for the five to 10s, 41 per cent of foster placements were considered to have been very helpful, whereas

Table 8.2

'Successful' and 'unsuccessful' endings, by age comparison of foster home and residential placements

	Age 5–10		Age 11+	
	Foster home	Residential	Foster home	Residential
N =	866	328	1062	3309
'Successful'	62%	61%	46%	44%
'Unsuccessful'	14%	9%	25%	17%
'Mixed'	24%	30%	31%	39%

only 29 per cent of residential placements came into this category. The gap closes if very helpful and fairly helpful are combined and 76 per cent of each type of placement scored very or fairly helpful. There is a much larger difference in the helpfulness scores for 11 + endings since 44 per cent of 11 + foster placements were felt to have been very helpful, compared with 23 per cent of the residential placements. When very and fairly helpful are combined, the gap widens for this age group and 81 per cent of foster placements compared with 67 per cent of residential score very or fairly helpful. We wondered if this was due to the inclusion of a large group of long-term foster placements but it was not so. The difference is just as evident in the placements which began and ended during the project.

Some insight into the differing scores on very helpful can be found in a study by Colton[11] comparing care practice in specialist foster homes and Children's Homes. Foster homes were found to be significantly more child oriented than the residential establishments which provided less individual attention.

So, to sum up, we can say that foster placements are considerably more prone to end prematurely, but provided they can be maintained, they usually meet their aims and are considered helpful. Residential placements carry less risk of premature ending but may last without achieving their aims and are less often perceived by social workers as having been very helpful.

These findings are in line with the general proposition made by Roy

Parker (quoted by Colton). He suggests that foster care involves high risks but can produce high benefits, whereas residential care carries lower risks but also lower benefits.

References

1 Prosser H *Perspectives on residential care* NFER, 1976.

2 Fuller R *Issues in the assessment of children in care* National Children's Bureau, 1985.

3 Tizard B *Adoption: a second chance* Open Books, 1977.

4 Triseliotis J and Russell J *Hard to place* Heinemann, 1983.

5 Rutter M, Quinton D and Liddle C 'Parenting in two generations' in Madge N (ed) *Families at risk* Heinemann, 1983.

6 Berridge D *Children's homes* Blackwell, 1985.

7 DHSS *Social work inspection of community homes*, 1985.

8 Davis A *The residential alternative* Tavistock, 1981.

9 House of Commons Social Services Committee on Children in Care, second report, 1984.

10 Millham S, Bullock R, Hosie K and Haak M *Lost in care* Gower, 1986.

11 Colton M 'Substitute care practice' *Adoption & Fostering* 12 1, 1988.

9 Placements for older adolescents – lodgings, hostels and flats

Placements of older adolescents, those aged 16+, inevitably have different patterns from those of the 14-15 year olds. There is a lot of movement in this age group which accounted for only eight per cent of admissions but for 17 per cent of all placements. This is because in addition to the admission and move placements of the often very troubled and difficult 16 year olds coming into the care system, there were a significant number of moves among young people who were about to leave care and were moving into independent or semi-independent living arrangements.

In spite of the recent upsurge of interest and concern about young people leaving care, there seems to be very little statistical information about placements that bridge the gap between in care and out of care. So although our data on lodgings, hostels and flats or bed-sits are rather meagre, it seems important to report such findings as we have. They need to be read in conjunction with the findings on offenders because 41 per cent of admissions of young people aged 16+ were of those remanded in care by courts while waiting for their next court appearance and another four per cent were on care orders made in criminal proceedings.

Lodgings
National statistics show lodgings as making only a modest contribution to child placement resources. The DHSS return for 31 March 1985 shows that just over 2000 young people in care in England and Wales were living in lodgings. This is 2.7 per cent of all children in care.

In our project sample, lodgings took a slightly higher profile. There were 355 lodgings placements over the two year period. This is only four per cent of all placements but 14 per cent of placements of young people aged 16+ were in lodgings. The 355 placements in lodgings were not proportionately spread across the authorities. Midshire accounted for almost half of them. This authority has a quite large and well established assisted lodgings scheme. Lodgings accounted for

143

nine per cent of all Midshire's placements and for 34 per cent of their placements of young people aged 16+.

In spite of their professional fostering scheme, County also made substantial use of lodgings for its older teenagers and 22 per cent of County's 16+ placements were lodgings. In City and Disctict, lodgings were used for nine per cent and eight per cent of placements for the 16+ age group but in North Thames these placements dropped to four per cent and in South Thames to less than one per cent. At first it seemed that lodgings might be more readily available in rural areas since it was the two counties which made most use of them. However, we were told that almost all lodgings are found in towns. Scarcity of housing and the presence of many students in London may have some influence, but it seems that an authority's policies must play a major part in determining the scale of the service.

It has not been possible to undertake a detailed comparison of the characteristics of young people going into lodgings, specialist foster homes or other placements, but some points of interest emerged from the analysis. In 25 per cent of lodgings placements the young person involved was on an offender status order. This compares with ten per cent of offenders among those going into specialist foster homes, but the reported level of serious behaviour problems was very similar for both types of placement. More boys than girls go into lodgings. The gender ratio for lodgings placements was 57 per cent boys and 43 per cent girls, whereas for specialist foster placements, proportions of boys and girls were almost even.

As one would expect, the aim of lodgings placements was mainly 'bridge to independence'. In a few cases they provided an emergency 'roof'. They were used mainly for young people moving out of residential accommodation. In only 15 per cent of these placements had the young person previously been living at home and in only ten per cent in a foster home. Because lodgings placements are not very stable, one lodgings placement in five was a youngster moving from other lodgings.

Perhaps by their very nature, lodgings are seldom long-term placements. Only 11 per cent of those that ended during the project had lasted over a year and none longer than two years. Two placements out of five had lasted less than two months. This was often due to premature endings, for 40 per cent were reported as not having lasted as long as planned and 32% had not lasted as long as needed.

In almost two-thirds of endings (63%), social workers considered that the lodgings placement had been at least fairly helpful but fewer than half (47%) were considered to have met their aims. This means that lodgings have a rather low 'success' rate on the project criteria of lasting and meeting aims and only 41 per cent achieved 'successful' ratings. On the face of it, this would appear to be a rather discouraging picture but, as we have seen, specialist foster placements are also hard to maintain. In Midshire in particular, both fieldwork staff and managers are rather enthusiastic about their assisted lodgings scheme and are planning to expand it. They report that some young people much prefer the independence of lodgings to either foster home or residential care and consider that lodgings meet the needs of some very difficult youngsters as well or better than anything else that can be offered.

Hostels
In comparison with previous decades, hostels now seem to be rather seldom used but they still account for ten per cent of placements for older adolescents and in South Thames 18 per cent of placements of those aged 16+ were in hostels. City was the only other authority to use hostels to any appreciable extent so between them, City and South Thames made 178 out of the 249 hostel placements reported during this project.

We have few details about these placements, but they often appear to be 'last resort' placements for very difficult youngsters and few last for any appreciable time.

Own flats or bed-sits
Like hostels, placements in flats and bed-sits made up about 10% of placements for the 16+ age group but they were rather more evenly spread across the authorities. The range was from seven per cent in District and County to 14 per cent in City and North Thames.

If one constructs a hierarchy of 'successful' placements for adolescents, own flats and bed-sits share top position with foster home with relatives. Fifty-five per cent of these placements both lasted and achieved their aims. Since the aim was almost always bridge to independence, it was generally considered to have been met provided the placement held.

Stein and Carey's study *Leaving Care*[1] has highlighted the difficulties

145

and loneliness experienced by many young people trying to manage on their own and ill-prepared for the task. Our data provide some factual support for their findings in that only three per cent of our young people shared their accommodation with a sibling and nearly one in three (30%) of those living in flats and bed-sits were out of contact with their own family, seeing relatives only occasionally or not at all.

Almost one in four of the flat/bed-sit placements did not last as long as planned but the proportion said not to have lasted as long as needed was only one in five (19%). This means that own flat or bed-sit placements appeared to last better than any of the other placements which ended in adolescence. However, comparison with residential or foster care is not really fair since quite a number of the moves into flats occurred shortly before the young person's eighteenth birthday and discharge from care so that they did not have to last long before obtaining a satisfactory coding on the project questionnaire.

Out of 174 own flat endings, 19 were moves to residential or foster care and ten to penal establishments. Twenty-four were moves to other flats or bed-sits, eight youngsters went home and there were four miscellaneous endings. But the largest group, 109 (63%) left care for independence and thus fulfilled the bridging intention of the placement.

References

1 Stein M and Carey K *Leaving care* Blackwell, 1986.

10 Placement of offenders

In a survey such as this, the only way of distinguishing offenders from other young people in care is by their legal status. We defined 'offenders' as those on remand and on S.7(7) care orders after criminal proceedings. We also included those on care orders in civil proceedings for non-school attendance. We found the whole issue of offenders in the care system complicated because:

• Those with the legal status of offender are not by any means the only young people who have committed offences. Offenders may enter care under place of safety orders or care orders in civil care proceedings as well as through criminal proceedings. The concern felt by parents and social workers about young people's criminal behaviour lies behind many voluntary admissions and many youngsters admitted for other personal or family reasons are delinquent in their behaviour.

• Offenders may be placed in foster homes or children's homes and those sent to penal establishments are not limited to young people who are admitted to care as offenders. Such placements by courts may follow a series of placements in voluntary care or where the local authority has assumed parental rights.

• Legal status at admission further 'undercounts' the proportion of offenders in the care system because remands and 7(7) care orders are often made on young people who are already in care.

• Disposals made by juvenile courts vary from one area to another.[1]

Analysis and interpretion of our data are bedevilled by all these complexities plus some others. Quite a number of the young people in our study had overlaps in their legal status, for example when remands followed voluntary admissions. Our project coding system could only cope with one legal status for each placement and we are not entirely satisfied that dilemmas over coding were always resolved in a consistent manner.

In Chapter 8 we drew attention to the disproportionate number of observation and assessment centre and CHE placements attributable to City and to how this is linked with the large numbers of offenders which this authority has in care. In considering all the project findings on offenders, we have to remember that City accounts for nearly half (45%) of all project placements of young people on remand, for three out of four care orders for non-school attendance (76%) and for two out of five care orders made following criminal proceedings (41%). Thus the overall project data on offenders are bound to be heavily influenced by what goes on in City while numbers in the other five authorities are apt to fall too low for comparisons to be drawn. It seems that in City and District care is seen as an appropriate response to offending, whereas in other areas, the courts, police, schools and social services departments are moving away from this position.

We also feel constrained by limitations on our ability to put our data on offenders into context. As a team we did not have any special knowledge of current work with young offenders and we could not extend our enquiries to look in any depth at local services or relationships with courts, police or schools. For all these reasons, it seems best to present our findings on offenders and their placements without much comment or attempt at interpretation. Our findings on black youngsters with offender status are included in Chapter 12.

Remands
During the project's two years of fieldwork 405 young people were remanded to the care of our six authorities. Nine out of ten of them were boys, 57 per cent were aged up to 15 and 43 per cent were 16 year olds. Of these 405 remands, nearly a quarter were made on young people who were already in care, though this proportion varied from 12 per cent or 13 per cent (North Thames and Midshire) to 29 per cent (City).

Of those admitted on remand, more than a third (38%) had been in care on at least one previous occasion. And if we look at the group of young people remanded during the first year of the project, we find that 14 per cent of them had had at least one more remand before the project ended. However, young people on remand do not have many placements. Remands account for 17 per cent of all 11+ admissions during the project but for only 12 per cent of all 11+ placements. This is in strong contrast to young people on 7(7) care orders who account for only two per cent of 11 + admissions but for 13 per cent of placements. Young people on remand also leave care fairly rapidly, probably because their cases in court come up within fixed periods. More than one in three left care within a month and well over half (57%) within two months. Fewer than one in five (19%) of the youngsters who came into care on a remand in Year 1 were still in care at the end of the project compared with exactly one in three of all teenagers admitted at this time. (Of course, many of the 16 year olds who were remanded in the early months of the project would have 'graduated' out of the care system by project end and some of those who left care after a remand will have gone into the penal system.)

The majority of remand placements were in observation and assessment centres (28%) or CHE/YPCs (27%) with another 18 per cent in penal establishments, six per cent in secure units, nine per cent in children's homes and five per cent at home. The remaining seven per cent of remands were scattered across a variety of settings but included only six foster home placements (1%).

Analysis of the behaviour problems recorded at the start of remand placements produces the following incidence of problems: stealing was a serious problem in 57 per cent of placements, running away in 28 per cent, general unmanageability in 23 per cent, truancy in 18 per cent, drug, solvent or alcohol abuse in 14 per cent. (Some young people had several of these problems.) The incidence of these behaviours in the placements of those on 7(7) orders was very similar but marginally lower.

Care orders in criminal proceedings S7(7)

Although the number of these orders has declined,[2] there were 261 young people in the project sample who were subject to them. Only 38 youngsters were admitted under such an order during the project. Another 89 were already in care on a 7(7) order when the project started and had moves or discharges during the next two years. The rest had admissions during the project but under another legal status. There is of course much overlap between those experiencing remands and 7(7) orders.

In general, far fewer girls than boys are convicted for offences. We found few girls subject to 7(7) orders. There were only 19 girls out of the 261 young people on 7(7) orders in our sample (7%). We also found that more than half (55%) of these youngsters had been in care before.

149

The most noteworthy point about this group of 261 7(7) offenders is the very large number of move placements that they account for. We calculate that in the whole 11+ age group, almost one in five of the placements following a move in care was of a young person on a 7(7) care order. During the two years of our data collection these 261 young people had 717 placements while they were on 7(7) orders plus any previous placements on remand, place of safety, etc. (It has not been possible to disentangle the placements of those who had more than one legal status because of time and cost constraints and the coding problems mentioned above.)

Care orders for Non-School Attendance (NSA)
In *Receiving juvenile justice,*[3] Parker, Casburn and Turnbull discuss the complex relationship of justice and welfare and the way in which care orders may carry what they describe as a 'hidden agenda'. Care orders made as a result of criminal proceedings may be seen by the young people concerned as punishment for an offence, but should be the result of an assessment of the youngster's needs and problems. They go on to say: 'This same process often occurs with education care proceedings because truancy is easy to prove . . . The number of adolescents in care for non-school attendance is no reflection of the reality of truancy nor are those in care with that legal status attachment there simply because of their refusal to go to school. They are selected for particular reasons.' This is, of course, the authors' gloss on the law which clearly states that there must be a need for care and control as well as truancy before a care order can be made. It seems that some courts – City's would clearly be one – consider that failure to attend school is itself evidence of a need for care and control. (Because of the distorting effect of an unusually large number of NSA admissions in the City, it was decided to omit 215 City cases where the only admission was for NSA. We understand that City is no longer accepting care orders for non-school attendance and will be closing one of its observation and assessment centres).

We have no means of proving what proportion of educational care orders in our sample used the fact of truancy as a means of getting a child into care, but some pointers emerge from our data. We can see that, with the exception of City, courts and authorities use this route into care very sparingly. During the two years of the project there were only 44 children who had admissions under care orders for NSA. Thirty of them came from City so that the other five authorities had only 14 between them. However, if young people are admitted to care on these orders, they quite often stay in care a long time. Of those admitted on care orders for NSA in Year 1, 38 per cent were still in care when the project ended. We also have in our sample 73 youngsters on these orders who were in care when the project started, had one or more moves during the project and were still in care when it ended two years later. A third pointer to the overlap between the truancy and other problems can be found in data from City where 116 non-school attenders had all had additional admissions for other reasons.

Yet another indicator of additional difficulties comes from the 'serious' behaviour problems reported at the start of placements on orders for NSA. Since some time may have elapsed between the making of an NSA order and the placement being reported on, it may not be too surprising that in only 41 per cent was truancy said to be a 'serious' problem. It may be more noteworthy that running away and stealing were both said to be a serious difficulty in 16 per cent of NSA placements, drug, solvent or alcohol abuse in nine per cent and 'general unmanageability' in 12 per cent.

The propensity of care orders to remain in force long after the original reasons for them have gone or been superseded by other problems is shown by some of the placements occurring under NSA orders. Of the 306 placements with this legal status, 134 (43%) were in children's homes, observation and assessment centres or CHE/YPCs and 105 (34%) were placements home on trial. However, there were 19 placements in lodgings, 14 in flats or bed-sits, ten in a hostel, eight in penal establishments and five in a secure unit. Interestingly, there was only one placement in an ordinary boarding school.

Young people in penal establishments
For those of us not recently working with young offenders in the care system, the number of young people sent by courts to penal establishments came as quite a shock. Six per cent of all teenage placements during the project were in detention or remand centres run by the prison service. They were spread fairly evenly across the six authorities with a range from four per cent in Midshire and County to seven per cent in City.

There were 183 boys and eight girls. These 191 young people had 330 penal establishment placements between them. All but 20 placements were moves in care. Sixty-two were moves between penal establishments, in 64 cases the youngster had been at home on trial or living independently and 14 came from foster homes. The largest group (170) were moves from local authority residential establishments.

Three out of four placements were remands in care or 7(7) care orders, but what appears to be a downward spiral of some youngsters in care is demonstrated by our finding 12 placements of young people still in voluntary care according to the completed questionnaires, five placements where the local authority had assumed parental rights and 38 under care orders made in civil proceedings. An alternative explanation is that a voluntary admission or admission through care proceedings masked an earlier pattern of offending.

The most usual length of penal establishment placements was two to six months (42%) but a third lasted less than a month, 17 per cent one to two months and ten per cent lasted more than six months. At the end of these placements about equal numbers went home or back to local authority residential care. About one in five placements ended with a move to another penal establishment, a few young people (9%) were discharged from care while still in custody, seven per cent moved to flats or lodgings and fewer still (2%) went on to foster homes. Just three young people went from penal establishments to bed and breakfast accommodation.

References

1   Richardson N *Justice by geography* Social Information Systems, 1987.

2   Morris A and Giller H *Understanding juvenile justice* Croom Helm, 1987.

3   Parker H, Casburn M and Turnbull D *Receiving juvenile justice* Blackwell, 1981.

11 Home on trial

The legal/administrative category 'home on trial' covers a wide variety of children's situations. Until now, little has been known about these placements for the only published research is Thoburn's *Captive clients*.[1] This was an in-depth, non-statistical study based on interviews with families and social workers. Research currently being undertaken at the University of Bristol by Professor Roy Parker and Elaine Farmer should do much to remedy this deficiency, but in the meantime our project provides basic information on the home on trial starts and endings in our six authorities.

In the period 1985/87, there were 859 home on trial placements. They form nine per cent of all placements but they are unevenly distributed across our six authorities and between age groups. In Midshire, home on trial accounted for 11 per cent of all placement starts whereas in North Thames it accounted for only six per cent and in County only seven per cent.

Table 11.1

Age at placement home on trial, by authority

	All	City	District	Mid-shire	County	North Thames	South Thames
N =	859	327	54	213	120	68	77
% of all placement starts	9%	9%	8%	11%	7%	6%	9%
0–4	17%	11%	9%	31%	14%	19%	10%
5–10	12%	8%	11%	16%	14%	18%	9%
11–13	12%	10%	13%	14%	8%	12%	16%
14–15	33%	41%	31%	24%	32%	19%	38%
16+	27%	30%	35%	14%	33%	32%	27%

Midshire also differs from the other project authorities in that 31 per cent of its home on trial placements concerned pre-school children whereas the average is 17 per cent. In most of our authorities, home on trial placements were primarily used for adolescents. This shows up clearly in Table 11.1 where 72 per cent of all placements can be seen to fall into the 11 + age band. In fact, in City, District, County and South Thames two thirds of all home on trial placements were young people of 14 upward. Further investigation of our figures disclosed that it was these older teenagers who were most likely to have had several placements at home on trial during the project. We understand that the Bristol University research findings show a more even age-spread in the four authorities they studied, so it seems that there is considerable variation in practice about how home on trial is used and Midshire may not be so unusual.

What Table 11.1 does not show is that home on trial placements are used for boys more often than for girls. Across all types of placements, the gender split is 59 per cent boys and 41 per cent girls. For home on trial it is 66 per cent to 34 per cent. This difference is almost entirely to be found in the adolescent age band. No less than 71 per cent of all teenagers going home on trial were boys, whereas for pre-school children the gender split is exactly 50 per cent to 50 per cent. This is, of course, linked with the frequent use of home on trial placements for offenders, since far more boys than girls are in care as a result of offending.

In 51 per cent of the teenage placements home on trial, the young person was on remand or subject to a care order which was for non school attendance or made during criminal proceedings. Of course this did not apply to the younger children, but a substantial proportion of the under 11s were wards of court or in care as a result of Matrimonial or Guardianship orders.

About half (48%) of all those going home on trial were leaving a residential establishment and a quarter (26%) were leaving foster homes. For 65 children (8%) the placement was a technicality in that they never physically left home but were allowed to remain under a changed legal status. A slightly larger group (10%) were returning home from a penal establishment.

The social workers completing our questionnaires selected care and upbringing as being the primary aim for the majority of home on trial placements in all age groups. However, for 27 per cent of pre-schoolers and 31 per cent of under 11s the aim was treatment or assessment and for 26 per cent of adolescents the aim was bridge to independence.

Outcomes

The expected end to a home on trial placement would normally be the formal discharge of the order, but we found that only one in four (24%) ended this way. In another 11 per cent, the order lapsed because the young person became 18. Almost one child in three (30%) moved back into residential care and another 14 per cent, mostly younger children, moved to foster homes. Fifty-five older adolescents (7%) moved to lodgings, bedsits or their own flat and 62 (8%) went to penal establishments. This left six per cent with a variety of other moves and endings.

Some of the moves into flats or bedsits were no doubt part of normal progress to independence and some of the 'other' moves were probably not due to breakdown of the home on trial arrangements. But even when these are put together with leaving care at 18 and the discharge of the care order, there are still the moves to foster homes, residential care or penal establishment which together add up to 52 per cent.

This ties in very closely with the response to the question about whether the placement had lasted as planned. Fifty-three per cent of the cases where there had been a plan were coded as not having lasted. The proportion coded as not having lasted as long as needed is considerably lower at 35 per cent which at first sight is somewhat perplexing. However, some explanations begin to emerge when we bear in mind the various reasons for using home on trial placements, including the need to allow the child or young person to go home and experience some of the problems before being ready to settle down elsewhere.

There was virtually no difference between the age groups in the proportion of placements which failed to last as long as needed but the five to tens were the most problematic on several counts. They had the highest proportion of endings occurring sooner than planned (51 per cent compared with 44 per cent for both under fives and 11 +). The five to tens also had the lowest score for the helpfulness of the placement. Only 60 per cent of their home on trial placements were coded as very helpful or fairly helpful compared with 70 per cent for both the pre-school and adolescent age groups. Apart from penal placements, home on trial placements have the lowest score for helpfulness.

As mentioned earlier in this chapter, care and upbringing was the aim for the majority of home on trial placements. In about half (48%) of these care and upbringing cases the aim was said to have been met fully or in most respects. In the next largest group (bridge to independence) the aim was fully or mostly met in only 33 per cent. One cannot help wondering how many of these had been 'last resort' placements of young people who had failed in other, in-care placements.

It is interesting to find that the aim of assessment which is difficult to achieve in many placements, notably in fostering, was achieved in nearly two thirds (64%) of placements home on trial. This held good for adolescents as well as younger children.

When all aims are grouped together the proportion of home-on-trial placements in which they were fully achieved is only 18 per cent. Another 29 per cent achieved the aim at least in most respects, giving a total of 47 per cent with aims fully or mostly met. Only lodgings placements have such a low score for achieving aims. However, it is necessary to bear in mind that very few home on trial placements have the relatively easy aims of temporary care or emergency 'roof' so the overall comparisons are somewhat misleading.

Similar considerations apply to comparisons of the 'success' of home-on-trial placements. On the face of it, home on trial would seem to be the least 'successful' of placement options. Overall, only 36 per cent of the 785 home on trial endings were said to have both lasted as needed and met their aim at least in most respects. Once again, the younger children's placements were the most 'successful' (46 per cent of under fives), and the 14-15 year olds had the least 'success' (23%). We understand that the preliminary findings from the Bristol study also show many premature endings, so the picture does indeed look rather gloomy. However, we believe that our figures need careful interpretation.

In the first place, the pattern of 'success' is very uneven. Although overall, the younger children's placements were the most likely to succeed, this was not so in all authorities. In City, only 13 per cent of home on trial endings of the five to ten age group were 'successful' compared with 60 per cent of under fives and 28 per cent of teenage endings. In District, not one of the nine home on trial placement endings of under tens was successful whereas their success rate for placements ending when the child was over 11 years old rose to 31 per cent. In County and North Thames, too, the percentage of successful placements rose with age. By contrast, Midshire not only returned far more young children home on trial than any other authority, it also had a high proportion of success with them (54 per cent of under fives and 50 per cent of five to tens). For reasons which are not clear to us, there are much greater differences between the six authorities' 'success' rates for home on trial than for foster home or residential placements. District with 27 per cent and City with 28 per cent home on trial 'successes' had the lowest percentages, while Midshire's score was 48 per cent.

There are also important, underlying considerations. We know from practice what our survey data cannot show, namely that some proportion of home on trial placements are undertaken without any great hope of success on the part of social workers, but because it is important for parents and child to have another opportunity to try and live together. A failure to achieve this may enable them to accept that a long-term in-care placement is necessary or may produce evidence on which such a plan can be based. Thus an assessment aim may be met even though, at another level, the placement did not last as long as the child needed it. We also know that placements at home may be a last resort because of lack of alternatives. These various factors no doubt account for our finding that one in four of these placements was coded 'doubtful' or 'inappropriate'.

Another point which needs to be borne in mind is the probable difference in the level of preparation and support given to home on trial placements as compared with foster placements though again this is a matter of practice knowledge rather than research findings.

References

1   Thoburn J *Captive clients* RKP, 1980.

12 Black children in care

The current lack of information about black children in care is serious and startling. There are no national statistics and few local studies, even though concern was expressed 20 years ago about what already appeared to be disproportionately large numbers of black children in the London care system.[1] Concern has continued ever since, most recently in the 1984 report of the House of Commons Select Committee on Children in Care.[2] Surveys in some individual local authorities have confirmed the presence of large numbers of black children in their care. For instance, research in Lambeth in 1982 showed that 49 per cent of children in care were black compared with 36 per cent in Lambeth as a whole. Five years earlier, Knight[3] had said 41 per cent of children in Lewisham's children's homes were black. However, Batta and Mawby[4] showed that in relation to the size of the Asian population in Bradford, Asian children were grossly under-represented among the children in care there.

Until now, studies have concentrated on the number of black children in care at a given point in time. This, of course, is not the same thing as the admission rate. If black children are disproportionately represented in the care system, we need to know whether this is because more black children are admitted, or because they stay in care longer thus gradually building up to a disproportionately large group. Our project provides the opportunity to take a close look at the admission rate and turnover of black children in care and also to seek answers to certain important questions. Are black children more likely than white children to have compulsory admissions? Do they experience different sorts of placements? Are those coming into care mainly teenagers or younger children? Are black children more often placed as sibling groups?

Black issues and the project's methodology
At the time the project authorities were chosen, we were not yet fully aware of the potential importance of our ethnic data and paid only

limited attention to the composition of the ethnic minorities in each authority. We find ourselves with quite a good balance of authorities with large or small ethnic minority populations, but we do not have an equivalent to Bradford where Asians form a very large minority group. There are substantial numbers of Asians in both our London boroughs and the work of Batta and Mawby enables us to check and compare our Asian data with theirs, but we are not able to take account of the important economic, religious and cultural differences within the Asian communities. We are aware that these differences could invalidate comparisons between authorities. The child care picture in an authority with many middle-class Ugandan Asians is likely to be very different from that in an authority with a large population of Bangladeshis working in low-paid jobs and living in bad housing conditions.

Many people strongly urged us to extend our enquiries to cover the ethnic background of care-givers and social workers as well as the children. We entirely understood the reasons for this pressure and shared the concerns about trans-racial foster and adoptive placements, the lack of black residential and field staff and the possible biases and misperceptions of white workers dealing with black children and their families. But to do justice to these issues would have involved adding not just one or two, but a substantial number of items to an already fairly lengthy questionnaire. It would also have added two complex extra dimensions to the analysis. We regretfully concluded that we could not stretch our resources to do the job properly. Trans-racial placements and unacknowledged racism in social workers and others are issues that are too important for anyone to be satisfied with the superficial treatment which would have been all that this project could have provided. In depth research on them is still urgently needed.

There was also considerable debate about how the various ethnic minorities were to be classified in the questionnaires. Our problems were compounded by the conflicting views of some of those whom we approached for advice. In the end, we decided to borrow the classification in use by BAAF member agencies when referring children to the Exchange. In spite of known defects, this classification had the merit of being already familiar and accepted. Once our Black Issues Advisory Group was established, it helped us to decide how best to combine some of the small sub-groups for analysis. The majority of the Group also strongly advised that we use the term 'black' to cover all children other than white.

For the purposes of this study, all Europeans, including Turkish and Greek Cypriots, have been coded as 'white', Asians from India, Pakistan and East Africa are all coded 'Asian' and 'other' includes Chinese, Japanese and Polynesians. For analysis, all children with one white parent and one black parent are considered to be of 'mixed parentage'. Sometimes, Africans and Afro-Caribbeans are also grouped together because the small number of Africans can make sensible comparisons difficult. Where it has seemed helpful, we have considered them separately. (As it happened, the number of Asian children in our sample was too small to have permitted further analysis by sub-group. But we now recognise that the initial classification could helpfully have included sub-divisions, for example Bangladeshis and Pakistanis and children of mixed black parentage, Afro-Caribbean/ Asian.)

For the rest of this chapter, we refer to six groups: Afro-Caribbean, African, Asian, white, mixed parentage and 'other'/not known. Eleven children were coded 'other' and proved to be mainly Chinese. The 'not-knowns' comprise five children where social workers failed to code ethnic origin and 74 cases where the respondent coded 'unknown'. These came mainly from City and were young offenders. In this authority probation officers may continue to carry responsibility for youngsters already under their supervision so staff in the SSD area offices sometimes had very little information on these cases although they were technically in care.

Synopsis
Our findings on black children in care are difficult to present and to follow because of the need to make so many comparisons, across ethnic groups as well as between age bands and authorities. Some of our findings are unexpected and run counter to commonly held assumptions. So it may help to state the main points right at the start.

• Project data confirm that black children were disproportionately represented in admissions to care. (They formed 17 per cent of project admissions.) However, we found that this was mainly accounted for by the large number of young black children being admitted for temporary care during family emergencies. They were admitted voluntarily, stayed only a short time and went home again.

● Mixed-parentage children, especially pre-schoolers, had a particularly high admission rate but their in-care patterns were more like those of white children and they stayed longer than Afro-Caribbean, African or Asian children.

● Adoption or a long-term foster placement was planned for about ten per cent of mixed-parentage children, but for hardly any children from the other black groups.

● In general we found unexpectedly few differences in either placement patterns or outcomes for black children when compared with white children. Somewhat greater differences were observed between the ethnic minority groups, but numbers were often too small for confident comparisons to be made.

Admission rates
Over the two years, 3748 children had 4682 admissions between them. (In this chapter we use data from both years whenever possible in order to get maximum numbers in the various sub-groups.) The first pie chart below shows the distribution of children across all ethnic groups. The second shows more clearly how the black children in our sample are distributed between the ethnic minorities and highlights the large proportion of children of mixed parentage being admitted to care.

Figure 12.1
Ethnic origin of children admitted to care 1985–7
N = 3748

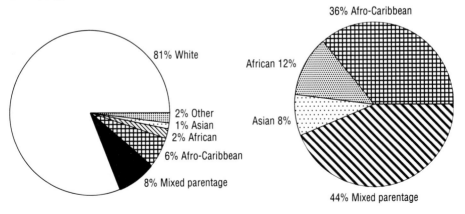

161

As one would expect, there were big differences between the six authorities in regard to the proportions of black and white admissions. The bar charts show how this varied from three per cent of black admissions in District to 51 per cent in South Thames, but it is noteworthy that some black children were admitted in every authority.

Figure 12.2
Admissions to care by ethnic origin and authority

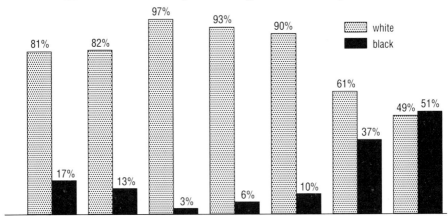

N =	4682	1601	315	930	823	594	420
	All	City	District	Midshire	County	Nth Thames	Sth Thames

Although it is instrinsically interesting, this information is of relatively little value without accurate information on the ethnic composition of the child population in each authority. Regrettably, such information is scarce and difficult to use for our purposes. There are two main sources. The first is the 1981 census which does not record ethnicity as such but rather the country of birth of the head of household. The relevant figures are set out below, but they almost certainly under-represent the proportions of black children in each authority. This is because the NCWP (New Commonwealth and Pakistan) group excludes the very significant number of children born to 'Black British' parents. (The Policy Studies Institute survey of 1984 reported that over ten per cent of the black householders who responded to the survey reported that they were born in the UK. This proportion of Black British parents will steadily increase as young

162

people born here start their families.)

The second source of information is data kept by local education authorities on the ethnic and cultural background of the school population. We have obtained some details from ILEA, from other education authorities and from ethnic minorities units in local authorities, but these are variable in quantity and quality. The education authority figures are likely to be much more accurate than the census data but of course they do not cover the pre-school age group.

An additional problem in assessing the proportional representation of black children in care is the lack of any demographic data on children of mixed parentage. Common sense and personal observation lead one to conclude that these children must be greatly over-represented in admissions to care as they form the largest sub-group of black children. This may seem quite startling but other studies have also pointed to the disproportionate number of mixed parentage children in care. [4,5]

Table 12.1 sets out the best available estimates of the proportion of black children in each of the participating authorities. In City and in North and South Thames it is possible to separate the NCWP group into Asian, Afro-Caribbean and African. Important differences are then revealed. In the London boroughs, especially South Thames, the majority of black children is of Afro-Caribbean or African origin whereas Asians form the largest black group in City. In the other three authorities this information is not available. The figures for project admissions to care are given in brackets.

Table 12.1 shows that black children were over-represented in admissions to care of all six project authorities, although the extent to which this was happening varied considerably. Equally important are the marked differences between the minority groups. When all these aspects are brought together, the admission patterns emerge.

Unlike other black children, Asian children were under-represented in each of the authorities where details are available, and in all age groups. Indeed admission rates for Asian children were less than one quarter of the white rate. In South Thames, where ILEA figures show Asian children forming 13 per cent of the primary school population and ten per cent in secondary schools, they accounted for just one per cent of this authority's admissions to care.

African and Afro-Caribbean children were over-represented particu-

Table 12.1

Approximate ethnic composition of child population and admission to care

	City	North Thames	South Thames	District	Mid-shire	County
UK/Irish/Greek/ Turkish/other white European	92% (82%)	63% (61%)	62% (49%)	97.5% (97%)	95% (93%)	94% (90%)
NCWP	8%	*	*	2.5%	5%	4%
Indian, Pakistani Bangladeshi	4% (1%)	8% (2%)	10% (1%)	** (2%)	** (–)	** (2%)
Afro-Caribbean	2% (3%)	10% (16%)	18% (26%)	** (–)	** (2%)	** (2%)
African	– (–)	3% (8%)	5% (8%)	** (–)	** (–)	** (1%)
Other/rest of world/NK	2% (5%)	16% (2%)	5% (2%)	** (–)	** (1%)	2% (–)
Mixed parentage	** (9%)	** (12%)	** (14%)	** (1%)	** (4%)	** (5%)

*Not applicable
**Information not available.
(Figures in brackets are project admissions)

larly in the pre-school and five to ten age groups where their admission rates were more than twice that of white children. African teenagers continued to be over-represented, especially in North Thames, but Afro-Caribbean teenagers entered care at only slightly higher rates than their white contemporaries.

We have already referred to the remarkably high overall admission rate for children of mixed parentage. This occurred in all age groups but particularly amongst pre-schoolers. The mixed parentage children accounted for no less than 13 per cent of all City's pre-school admissions, 16 per cent in North Thames and 19 per cent in South Thames.

When the authorities' figures for admissions of mixed parentage children are examined individually, interesting differences can be seen. In areas with large black populations such as our London boroughs, mixed parentage children accounted for less than half of black admissions to care. But in City and Midshire where black people account for a smaller proportion of the population, the majority of black children admitted to care proved to be those of mixed parentage. We have no adequate explanation for this and can only speculate about possible lack of family and community support for 'mixed' families in these areas. The lack of demographic data makes it impossible to know whether such variations are in line with the numbers of mixed parentage children in the population.

Age at admission

The large number of pre-school admissions in all authorities has been noted in earlier chapters. It is an even more prominent feature of black admissions. Forty per cent of black admissions were in the under five age group compared with 35 per cent white. Within the ethnic minority groups there are also noticeable differences. Whereas the years under five account for between 30 per cent of admissions of Afro-Caribbean children and 38 per cent of admissions of African children, only 19 per cent of Asian admissions were pre-schoolers. Correspondingly, Asians had the highest proportion of children aged five to 13 at admission. Africans had many under fives but relatively few young people coming into care in their mid to late teens. The Afro-Caribbean age curve is very similar to that of whites as Figure 12.3 demonstrates. What is interesting is that, contrary to popular perceptions, there is no big bulge of Afro-Caribbean adolescents being admitted to care. Once again, it is the mixed parentage children who stand out as different. In every authority about half of all mixed parentage admissions were in the under five group.

Plan at admission

Analysis of answers to the question 'What is the overall plan for this child now?' shows that, at admission, proportionately more children of Afro-Caribbean (58%), African (66%) and Asian (62%) origin were expected to return home. The equivalent figure for white children was only 48 per cent. Mixed-parentage children, with 52 per cent expected to go home, were once again more like the whites.

Adoption was planned for just four Afro-Caribbeans, one African

165

Table 12.2

Admissions to care, by ethnic group

	All	White	Afro-Carib	African	Asian	Mixed parent	Other/ NK
N =	4683	3783	285	88	52	367	108
0–4	35%	35%	30%	38%	19%	53%	20%
5–10	20%	20%	30%	25%	36%	18%	14%
11–13	14%	14%	11%	19%	23%	9%	9%
14–15	23%	23%	21%	12%	10%	12%	38%
16+	7%	8%	8%	6%	12%	8%	19%

Figure 12.3
Age distributions of different ethnic groups

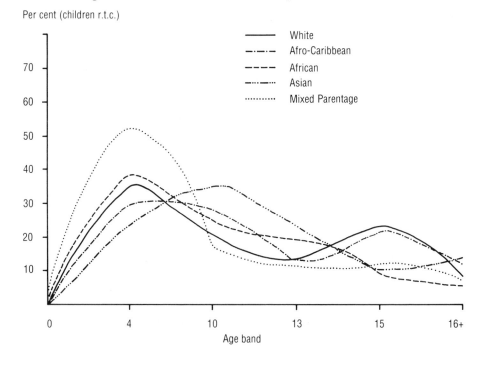

Per cent (children r.t.c.)

White
Afro-Caribbean
African
Asian
Mixed Parentage

Age band

and one Asian, all of them less than five years old. In strong contrast, adoption was the plan for 25 mixed parentage pre-schoolers and two older children. This is seven per cent of all mixed-parentage children and compares with five per cent of white admissions where adoption was planned from the start.

There are indications from our figures that though very few young Asian children come into care, those who are admitted are more often expected to remain. But Asian teenagers in the project were more likely than other adolescents to have their return home planned right from the time of admission. Across all the age groups 13% of Asians were expected to remain in care and a similar proportion of whites. Nine per cent of mixed parentage children, but only seven per cent of Afro-Caribbean and six per cent of Africans had 'remain in care' as the plan at admission.

Aim of placement
Several times already during this report we have drawn attention to the strong association between placement aims and placement outcome. Aims are also closely linked with legal status, overall plans and expected length of stay. As we have seen, black children were more often admitted voluntarily for short periods and more often expected to return home again, so it is not surprising to find that 'temporary care' was much the most frequently recorded aim for black children. It was the aim for one in three placements for white children but for about half the placements of Afro-Caribbean, Asian and mixed parentage children and two-thirds of the placements of African children.

Differences between the ethnic groups were most pronounced in the admissions of younger children which has obvious practice implications in terms of the need for black, short-stay foster homes. While this was a feature of admissions in most of the study authorities, it was particularly striking in our London boroughs. In North Thames, black children accounted for 48 per cent of temporary care admissions in the under 11 age group. In South Thames this rose to 61 per cent. Looking back to Table 12.1, we can roughly calculate that, in these boroughs, almost twice as many young black children were admitted for temporary care as would be expected from their numbers in the population.

The picture is different for adolescents. As the figure below makes clear, the proportion of black teenagers admitted for temporary care

Figure 12.4
Percentage of admissions where aim is temporary care, by ethnic group and age

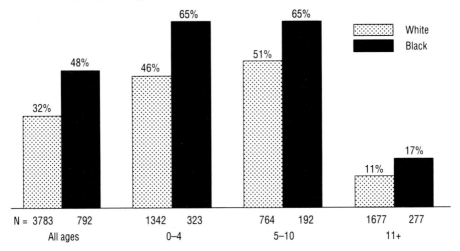

was only marginally higher than for white adolescents.

Our data do not enable us to offer explanations about why black families with young children need/use temporary care more frequently than white families. More single parent families and harsh socio-economic pressures no doubt enter into it. But Batta and Mawby suggest that black families may use the care system as a replacement for an extended family and many would agree that this is how community care should be used. The current study of children entering care by the Personal Social Services Research Unit at the University of Kent should provide some much needed information on ethnic differences.

Legal status
When we start to look at the project children by legal status as well as by age and ethnic group, numbers sometimes fall too low for reliability, especially in the small Asian group, but the general picture comes through clearly. Young black children were more likely than young white children to be admitted to care voluntarily while for adolescents the ratio of voluntary to compulsory admissions was almost identical. Fifty-eight per cent of the admissions of white adolescents were

voluntary as were 56 per cent of admissions of black. This pattern holds good across all authorities in spite of the variations in policy and court practice which have been mentioned in previous chapters.

Figure 12.5
Percentage of voluntary admissions, by ethnic group and age

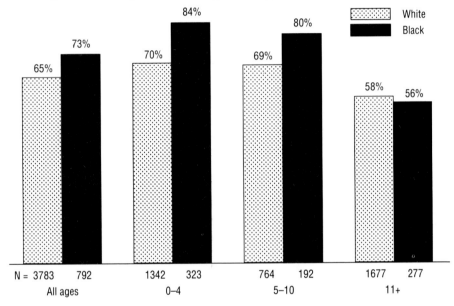

A close look at compulsory admissions shows up interesting details. In comparison with whites, only about half as many young black children were admitted on place of safety orders. Mixed parentage children of all ages were the most likely to be on care orders through care proceedings. By contrast not one Asian child or young person was admitted on a care order. All compulsory admissions of Asians were place of safety orders or remands. Afro-Caribbean adolescents appear to have proportionately more remands to care than do white adolescents, but the majority of Afro-Caribbean remands in our sample came from just one authority, South Thames. It is noteworthy that whereas remands to care for black 14 and 15 year olds were almost twice as frequent as for their white contemporaries, this pattern is reversed for the young people aged 16+. Only 25 percent of our black adolescents aged 16+ came into care on remand compared with 42 per cent of whites. We surmise that older black teenagers may be remanded to the penal system and not into care, since several studies have expressed concern about over-representation of black youngsters in custody.[6, 7]

Type of placement
One has to look hard to find any differences at all between the basic types of placement used for white or black children. Where there do appear to be differences they are almost always accounted for by age or placement aim or some particular emphasis in an individual local authority.

There are four points of difference or similarity that need special mention.

● Slightly fewer black children went home on trial. (This is probably linked with the small proportion of black children on care orders.)

● Rather surprisingly, in view of concern about finding foster homes for black children, we found that fostering rates for white, Afro-Caribbean and mixed parentage children were almost identical. The proportion of Asian children fostered appears lower, but the numbers are so small that one or two families placed in children's homes could have a strong effect on percentage values. Knapp[8] found that in the authority he studied, black boys were less likely to be fostered than white boys.

● Proportionately more black teenagers went into specialist foster homes. This was not just because South Thames with a large specialist scheme also has many black adolescents in care. Even within South Thames, black youngsters were particularly likely to experience this type of placement

● When placement patterns of white and black offenders are compared, the percentage of placements in penal establishments are identical (6 per cent for both groups). However, within the black group, Afro-Caribbeans had a slightly higher proportion of penal establishment placements (8%) while the proportions for Asian and mixed youngsters were somewhat lower (four per cent and three per cent). In considering these findings it is essential to remember that this project can provide no information about young people who go to penal establishments without entering the care system, so our data on ethnicity and the placement patterns of offenders is very partial.

Family links
For all placement endings that occurred during the project, we have information on whether or not the child was placed with one or more siblings. Analysis shows that where there were siblings in care, Afro-Caribbean/African children were more likely to be placed together. We do not know whether white and mixed parentage families were more often split up at admission or whether children from these groups more often came into care at different times or were half siblings who did not even know each other. All we can say is that, when cases where there were no siblings in care have been excluded, 63 per cent of white and 65 per cent of mixed-parentage placements were with at least some siblings compared with 81 per cent Afro-Caribbean/African and 79 per cent Asian placements.

We also have some limited information on other family contact during placement. There is very little difference between the ethnic groups in terms of frequency of contact. The children most likely to have had placements in which there was no contact with their natural family were those of mixed parentage who were leaving foster homes. This can probably be accounted for by single mothers in hospital for illness or confinement and by there being quite a number of mixed parentage children in placements for adoption, but our data do not permit detailed analysis of this point.

Moves in care and re-admissions
In order to get a picture of moves and re-admissions over at least a 12 month period, it is necessary to limit the analysis to children admitted in the first year of the project. This of course reduces the numbers and makes detailed comparison less reliable. There were only 28 Asian children admitted during this period so extreme caution is needed in interpreting any apparent differences in their experiences.

Moves in care are bound to be strongly linked with aims of placement. For example, preparation for long-term placement pre-supposes a subsequent move and assessment is also frequently followed by a change of placement. Temporary care seldom involves such changes and, since this was the most usual placement aim for African and Afro-Caribbean children, one would expect them to have the fewest moves, as was indeed the case. Sixty-nine per cent of the Afro-Caribbean/African children had no moves compared with 56 per cent of white children. However, detailed analysis revealed that if Afro-Caribbean children moved at all, they were somewhat more likely to have had three or more moves and this seemed to occur across all age groups.

Moves for mixed-parentage children followed much the same pattern as for white children: 54 per cent of them had no moves, 31 per cent had one move, ten per cent two moves and five per cent three or more. Half the Asian children had no moves and the other half had one to three.

We saw in Chapter 3 on overall patterns of care, that re-admissions to care are quite a prominent feature of the child care system and of course they tend to be associated with temporary care rather than other placement aims. Although most of the 683 children who had an admission for temporary care in Year 1 were not re-admitted during the project, there were 51 (7%) who had at least two more temporary admissions (i.e. three or more admissions in all). Those most likely to have this experience were the pre-school, mixed parentage children. Out of 45 mixed parentage under fives admitted for temporary care in Year 1, eight (18%) had had at least three admissions before the end of the second year. The equivalent figure for white pre-school children is eight per cent and none of the Afro-Caribbean, African or Asian pre-schoolers had more than two temporary care admissions. The implications seem to be that an alarmingly high proportion of mixed parentage youngsters will experience multiple admissions during their childhood.

Length of time in care
On the whole, Afro-Caribbean/African children had shorter care episodes than other ethnic groups. Over half (56%) of their admissions lasted less than eight weeks. This compares with 50 per cent mixed parentage, 44 per cent white and 37 per cent of the small number of Asian admissions. However, when one looks at those which had lasted longer than six months, then the chances of remaining in care for more than a year look quite similar across the ethnic groups. Out of 166 care episodes of Afro-Caribbean/African children which started in Year 1 of the project, 47 (28%) were still continuing when the project ended, i.e. a year or more later. The equivalent percentage for mixed parentage

children is 27 per cent, for whites 32 per cent and for Asians 39 per cent, although Asian numbers are too small for reliable comparisons.

More detailed analysis shows that while Afro-Caribbean/African pre-schoolers very seldom had long spells in care (only 13 per cent were still in care a year or more later), the situation of Afro-Caribbean teenagers appears to be different, with 42 per cent reported to be still in care at least one year later, compared with 34 per cent of white teenagers. However, this difference is not statistically significant.

Outcomes
What we most need to know is whether, within similar placements and age groups, ethnic background affects outcome. To tease this out of a complex data set which was not specifically designed for this purpose is extremely difficult. There are many variables of age, ethnic group, placement type, length, aim, etc. to be considered. We found, too, that such a large proportion of the black children in our sample were young children having short placements for temporary care, that when we wanted to compare placements with other aims or those of older children, the numbers in each sub-group often become very small and so of questionable reliability. Nor have we had either the time or the resources to employ the sophisticated techniques that might be used for detailed comparative analysis. Our findings on outcome and ethnicity are therefore more tentative and limited than we would wish.

We also feel it necessary to be particularly cautious about our 'soft' data on placement outcomes for black children. We do not know how many of the social workers who completed the questionnaires were themselves black, whether the foster placements were same race or trans-racial, or whether there were black staff members in the residential establishments in which black children were placed. One can surmise that the shock of finding oneself cared for by adults with a different culture and life-style would add greatly to the trauma of short-stay placements of young children. The potential identity problems of black children brought up in white foster and adoptive families are now better understood. (These are helpfully summarised by Weise).[9] For all these reasons, we must emphasise that our crude categories of 'successful' and 'unsuccessful' placements have to be treated even more circumspectly when applied to children from ethnic minorities.

Nevertheless, the project has obtained some useful 'hard' data that has not previously been available. We can reach some general conclusions and can say with considerable confidence that, in many respects, outcomes for black and white children are essentially similar. We can also point to some interesting but more tentative differences which we hope others may be able to explore in greater detail.

'Success' rates

This chapter has emphasised major differences between ethnic groups in age distribution and placement aims. Many aspects of placement outcomes reflect these differences. For instance, we know from looking at overall outcomes that temporary care placements are usually successful in terms of lasting as needed and meeting this aim. They are brief and the children go home again. Earlier in this chapter we have seen that a higher proportion of young black children are placed for temporary care. So it is not particularly enlightening to report that more young black children have successful placements and return home quickly. It therefore makes sense to confine any comparison of overall 'success' rates to the 11+ group.

Looking across all types of placement, we find that slightly more black teenagers had 'successful' endings (45 per cent compared with 42 per cent white). Within the black group, Asian and mixed parentage teenagers had a somewhat higher proportion of 'successful' placements than did Afro-Caribbeans and Africans. When foster home and residential endings are compared, Afro-Caribbeans seem to have had high 'success' ratings for foster home endings and low ones for residential endings, whereas for Asians this pattern was reversed. However, numbers were too small for us to take account of different placement aims or differing placement patterns in authorities with high and low proportions of young black people in care so these findings must be treated with great caution.

Behaviour problems

When our data on problems in placement are considered by ethnic group, we find once again that it is similarities not differences that emerge. Caregivers were fractionally more likely to have found the behaviour of black children and young people unacceptable (20 per cent black, 18 per cent white). But when the incidences of particular behaviour problems are studied, the only item where black children scored higher by more than one or two percentage points was that Afro-Caribbean youngsters were more likely to have been considered 'withdrawn' (nine per cent compared with four per cent white and three per cent Asian or mixed parentage). Within the black group, African and Asian children had a lower reported incidence of almost all behaviour problems in comparison with those of Afro-Caribbean and mixed parentage background. A few examples will demonstrate the patterns.

Table 12.3

Incidence of behaviour problems, by ethnic group

	All	White	Afro-Carib.	African	Asian	Mixed parent	Other/NK
N =	9335	7648	583	107	93	753	147
Withdrawn	4%	4%	9%	2%	3%	3%	3%
'General unmanageability'	11%	12%	13%	3%	3%	12%	5%
Stealing	10%	10%	12%	2%	5%	9%	6%
Running away	9%	10%	7%	1%	9%	6%	0%

Foster placements
Within the foster placement group, black children were the most likely to have had very short placements and to have left in less than a week, but the proportions of black and white children whose placements had lasted for at least three years were exactly the same, ten per cent.

There was also a remarkable similarity across all ethnic groups in the proportions of foster placements which did or did not last as needed. The placements of Asians and mixed parentage children had a slightly greater tendancy to last 'too long', but the almost identical percentages of 'did not last as needed' is most striking.

When these figures are broken down into age bands, there is some indication that if placements of Afro-Caribbean, African and mixed parentage teenagers are going to end prematurely, this is most likely to occur in the early or middle years of adolescence whereas premature endings for whites continue on into the 16 + group. For example, out of

Table 12.4

How placement lasted, by ethnic group

	All	White	Afro-Carib	Asian	Mixed parent	NK
N =	3554	2813	315	29	342	55
Lasted as long as needed	66%	66%	68%	55%	66%	69%
Did not last as needed	24%	24%	23%	24%	23%	24%
Lasted too long	9%	9%	8%	14%	11%	7%
NK	1%	1%	1%	7%	–	–

27 endings of mixed parentage children who were then aged 14–15, no less than 17 (63%) were said not to have lasted as needed. This compares with 47 per cent of white youngsters in the same age band. Of placements which ended when the young person concerned was 16+ only 20 per cent mixed parentage placements had failed to last as needed compared with 30 per cent of whites' placements.

Similar, but slightly smaller differences can be found when Afro-Caribbean teenage foster endings are compared with white. In the white group, 47 per cent of 14-15 year old placements ended prematurely as did 30 per cent where the young person was 16+. The equivalent percentages for Afro-Caribbeans were 55 per cent and 16 per cent.

Placements of Afro-Caribbean/African teenagers which had the aim of treatment or assessment were the most prone to premature endings. Forty-two per cent of their placements failed to last as long as needed compared with 24 per cent white and 30 per cent of adolescents of mixed parentage who had had similar placements. There were too few Asian placements of this sort to include them in any comparisons.

Only minor differences can be found when circumstances of placement endings are compared across ethnic groups. Overall, a higher proportion of black children's placements end with a return home but Asian parents seem slightly more likely than other parents to remove their children against advice. Apart from this, similarities prevail as they have in other aspects of placement outcome.

References

1 Fitzherbert K *West Indian children in London* Bell, 1967.

2 House of Commons Social Services Committee on Children in Care, second report, 1984.

3 Knight L 'Giving her roots' *Community care*, 15 June 1977.

4 Batta I and Mawby R 'Children in local authority care. Monitoring racial differences in Bradford' *Policy and Politics* 9 2, 1981.

5 Rowe J and Lambert L *Children who wait* ABAFA, 1973.

6 Tipler J *Juvenile justice in Hackney* Hackney Social Services Department, 1986.

7 National Association for Care and Resettlement of Offenders *Grave care, grave doubts* NACRO, 1988.

8 Knapp M, Baines B and Fenyo A 'Consistencies and inconsistencies in child care placements' *British Journal of Social Work* 18 (supplement), 1988.

9 Weise J *Transracial adoption* Social Work Monograph 60 University of East Anglia, 1986.

13 Conclusions

We emerge from this study sadder and wiser but with a sense of accomplishment. We achieved our aims even if some things could not be done in the detail we would have wished. Our findings confirm and amplify the results of other recent studies, shatter a few myths and misconceptions, and cut down to size some claims about the scale of change and new developments. However, they also give some grounds for optimism and show that there have been some improvements in practice in recent years.

The children going into placements
Perceptions of social workers, managers and administrators about what is going on in child care are built up from a variety of sources. These include:- annual statistics; news and articles in professional journals; papers given at conferences; research reports; personal experience of one's own caseload or area. Any or all of these may provide a distorted or very limited picture.

Misperceptions may also arise because some children in care are much more visible than others. Whereas children and young people in foster homes or home on trial are scattered and seldom or never seen by senior social workers or managers, those in residential care have a much higher public profile and make their presence felt. Black youngsters in residential establishments are particularly 'visible'.

Just as some families consume a disproportionate amount of social work time,[1] so do some children in care. It may be the large amounts of social work time required to achieve older child adoption placements which in part accounts for the perception that these placements are far more numerous than they really are. Certainly the frequent moves of some adolescents (for example, those on 7(7) care orders) must contribute to the feeling that almost all children in care are teenagers.

In theory, everyone concerned with social services knows that there are big differences between departments. However, most people only have direct experience of a limited number of them and probably have only a vague idea about the overall patterns of resources or of the characteristics of children in care. Certainly we on the project research team were unprepared for the huge differences in style, policies, resources and placement patterns that emerged from our statistical data and from the descriptive study.

Among some generally held beliefs which our project data overturn are the following:

Belief: *The considerable reduction in the number of children in care signifies a major reduction in child care placement work.*

Finding

The project provides data on the rapid flow of children in and out of care which along with moves within the care system, builds up into a formidable number of placements. The amount of work which must have been involved for the six project authorities in the 9723 placement starts and 9335 endings which were monitored during the two year period, is really quite staggering. One gets little or no idea of it from year end statistics.

Belief: *The child care service is now mainly concerned with adolescents.*

Finding

Although year end statistics are indeed dominated by adolescents, this gives a somewhat misleading impression caused by the build-up of young people who have grown into adolescence while in long-term care. The reality is that it is in the first year of life that children are most vulnerable to admission to care. Many young children come into care but they stay for shorter periods than do the adolescents. Well over half of all admissions to the project authorities were children under 11 years old and more than a third were pre-schoolers.

Belief: *The residential sector has shrunk almost to nothing.*

Finding

The reduction in the number of residential places during the 1980s is a reality which cannot be gainsaid, but it is quite hard to reconcile with our finding that more than half of all teenage placements were in residential establishments as were one in four placements of the five to tens. We found that only 15 per cent of adolescent placements were in foster homes so one can only suppose that the reduction in residential places has been achieved through higher occupancy rates, shorter stays, more use of home on trial, hostels, flats and lodgings, as well as some modest increase in fostering for teenagers.

Belief: *Most fostering is now task centred with heavy emphasis on placement of teenagers.*

Finding

The day to day work of the fostering service is still heavily weighted toward temporary foster care for young children. Fifty per cent of all foster placements made by the project authorities were of children under five years old and only 35 per cent of all foster placements were task-centred. There probably have been considerable changes in the past decade but it is impossible to measure these because apart from the boarding-out percentages given in the DHSS return, there are no national figures on foster care.

Belief: *Long-term foster placements are a thing of the past.*

Finding

Long-term fostering is certainly not a thing of the past, but its focus has changed rather dramatically. Whereas previously it was predominantly a service for young children, the majority of new long-term foster placements now involve teenagers.

Belief: *Considerable numbers of older children are being placed for adoption.*

Finding

In view of all the emphasis on planning for permanence and on adoption as a resource for older children, it was quite astonishing to find that across all six authorities and over the whole two year period, only 40 of the 260 placements where the aim was adoption involved children over the age of five. Of these 40 cases, half came from just one authority so it seems that in most areas, adoption services are still virtually confined to placing babies and toddlers.

Belief: *Black children are disproportionately represented in the care system.*

Finding

The situation is complex and in some respects different from prevailing beliefs. This study confirms that Afro-Caribbean, African and mixed parentage children are disproportionately represented in admissions to care while Asian children are conspicuous by their absence. Contrary to expectations, the black youngsters entering care in the project authorities were not predominantly adolescents but young children needing only temporary care. Few young Afro-Caribbean, African or Asian children come into long-term care but mixed parentage children do, and are very much more likely than other black children to be placed for adoption.

The outcomes of various types of placement
There are fewer surprises in the project's findings on outcome but much more complexity. The main conclusions concern the difficulty and danger of making comparisons.

Factual findings include salutary reminders about the amount of movement in care. Nearly half of all placements ended with a move to another in-care placement. Many of these moves could be considered beneficial, for example, children going home on trial, infants going to adoptive families, older teenagers moving to their own accommodation. Nevertheless, the amount of dislocating change that children in care have to cope with is still a cause for serious concern. So is our finding that 25 per cent of adolescents' placements were said not to have lasted as long as needed.

Evidence from this study indicates that recent emphasis on planning and reviews has been effective in reducing placement drift and only a tiny proportion of the placements made in Year 1 of the project were seriously overdue at project end. (It is, of course, important to remember that drift in placement is not the same thing as drift in care which might include a series of placements.) Premature endings continue to be a serious problem especially for older children.

Both common sense and practice wisdom tell us that it is more difficult to sustain a long-term placement than one that is intended to be brief, so there are no surprises in the project findings on premature endings and length of stay. Nor is there anything new in our findings on the strong relationship between increasing age and an increase in placement breakdown. However, it may be necessary to emphasise the age factor because of its importance when comparing outcomes across authorities or between types of placement or when considering the breakdown rates found by various researchers.

What we do believe to be new and potentially useful, are our findings on the inter-relationships of placement aim and placement outcome along with age and length of stay. Classification of placements by aim helps to explain similarities and differences in outcome that are otherwise extremely puzzling. It is, of course, obvious that aims which are inherently difficult to achieve – for example, treatment – will be less often achieved than aims which are comparatively easy – for example, temporary care. But what has not always been fully appreciated, and what our data so clearly show, is that there can be a variety of aims within a particular age group, or type of placement or expected placement length and the degree of difficulty of the aim will affect the outcome.

Our findings show that although foster placements of teenagers are markedly less successful than those of pre-schoolers, teenage placements with the aim of temporary care meet this aim more often than do pre-school children's placements with difficult aims such as treatment. We find, too, that the category 'short-term fostering' may include placements with difficult aims as well as the easier ones of temporary care or 'roof over head'. Specialist fostering schemes include variable proportions of the easier and more difficult placement aims and so do placements with relatives. Similar variations are found within the residential sector.

A question which has troubled the research team and which we suspect will also arise in the minds of those reading this report is 'How should we regard the various levels of placement 'success' that the survey reveals?' We have to accept that the success measure is crude and says nothing about quality. A study of consumers' views would no doubt reveal different patterns. Nevertheless, no responsible profession can avoid concern about the results of its interventions and social work is becoming increasingly concerned with evaluations.

Overall, half of all placements which ended during the project were said to have been 'successful' in that they lasted as long as needed and met their aims at least in most respects. This overall figure masks a range from 60 per cent of foster placements to 46 per cent of residential placements and only 36 per cent of placements home on trial, but these comparisons in turn do not take account of age differences or placement aim. The patterns become complicated when these various factors are taken into account, but what is very evident is that 'success' rates for home on trial were low for all ages, and that in both fostering and residential care fewer than half of the task-centred placements with aims such as treatment, assessment or 'bridge to independence' succeeded. The aim 'care and upbringing' was also associated with a rather low percentage of 'successful' outcomes (43%).

It is difficult to know how to interpret these results because there are so few benchmarks against which to measure them. We do not know what proportion of home on trial placements were lasting or breaking down a decade ago and there have been no comparable studies of outcomes of residential care. When it comes to fostering, we do have other research findings to use as a yardstick and in previous chapters we have noted some encouraging signs of improvement in fostering practice that can be deduced from careful comparisons. It may well be that there has been equivalent improvement in other types of placement since the indications are that placement aims are set higher these days and more is expected. Perhaps some of the depression about current practice is because people are unaware that the goal posts have been moved.

Possible links between foster placements outcomes and the organisation of foster care services.
Some people will be disappointed with our finding that there appears to be no obvious and direct link between structure of the fostering service and overall outcome patterns. It may be daunting to have to accept the complex interactions which preclude easy solutions or comparisons, but it could also save disappointment if expectations of the benefits of re-organising structures can be reduced. The search for the perfect system is clearly fruitless.

Our exploration of the advantages and disadvantages of having specialist fostering staff and of the ways in which they can be deployed will, we hope, enable agencies to identify and counteract some of the inevitable disadvantages involved in any of the possible organisational patterns they may have at present or may introduce in the future.

Because this was essentially a quantitative and not a qualitative study, we could not attempt to investigate possible links between generic and specialist structures and the quality of each authority's foster care services. An in-depth study of social work input in the recruitment, assessment, preparation and support of foster placements is still greatly needed but would be methodologically difficult.

The viability, strengths and weaknesses of a monitoring system.
We showed that our system 'worked' and could be maintained even in the midst of departmental re-organisations but only if sufficient administrative resources are available. The fact that none of the six authorities was in a position to maintain the scheme after the end of the project makes us realise that at the outset we were unduly optimistic about the possibility of most present day social services departments being able to sustain routine monitoring except at the simplest level. We had over-estimated the departments' administrative resources and underestimated the complexity of the analysis.

With research sections and administrative support staff reduced to dangerously low levels, it now seems quite unrealistic to suppose that many departments could provide people to do the essential, continuous, routine tasks of collecting, chasing, checking and analysing data on placement outcome as a permanent feature of their work and without outside assistance, though a few, such as Strathclyde, Fife and Leicestershire, have managed it at least for a time. Awareness of the difficulties of introducing, maintaining, analysing and interpreting large-scale monitoring efforts will, we hope, save other departments from embarking on over-ambitious schemes which cannot be sustained and therefore only increase social workers' distrust of research and evaluation.

It is the evaluative component of monitoring that is difficult. The increasing use of computers for keeping child care statistics should make it relatively easy to keep track of child care placement patterns and to pick up samples for further study. This sort of monitoring is a useful first step toward more sophisticated evaluation.

The need for continued monitoring and evaluation of the outcomes of child care placements is urgent. It is frightening to think of the time and money expended on providing services without knowing whether or not they are helpful or effective. Even quite simple enquiries can be very helpful as reports such as the Barnardo's project reports have shown.

We plan to use the experience gained in our large-scale survey to produce a simplified version in the form of an outline and workbook for small-scale, time-limited monitoring exercises. These could be undertaken by project leaders, area directors, officers in charge of establishments and principal officers responsible for child care. Previous research and computer experience would not be necessary.

Implications for policy and practice

Implications for policy and practice do not readily emerge from a survey such as this but a few points can and should be made:

• The continuing propensity of placements of all kinds to come to a premature end is an indication that post-placement support should be high on the list of priorities.

• The failure of so many task-centred placements to meet their aims points to the importance of more joint training of social workers and caregivers and to the need for written agreements and more explicit aims and tasks.

• Home on trial placements appear to be in urgent need of more attention and resources both in preparation for the child's return home and subsequently.

• Since residential placements are still so extensively used, the importance of adequately resourced group care services for adolescents may need to be stressed. There seems to be a risk that residential services for children will receive insufficient attention from managers who may see them as an expensive liability whose decline should be hastened.

• Large numbers of young children are still experiencing placements away from home with all the distress and trauma that this may bring if insensitively handled. Yet little or no emphasis is given in social work training to the knowledge, skills and meticulous attention to detail required from foster parents and social workers dealing with these short-stay placements of pre-school children. Handling these placements could beneficially be considered a specialism in its own right.

• The large number of young black children admitted for temporary foster family care highlights the need for an adequate number of black foster parents from various ethnic minorities represented in each authority.

Further studies needed

It was always our hope that this study would provide a factual base on which other research could be developed and the data are stored at the ESRC Data Archive, University of Essex, Colchester. We now realise

185

that our sample offers ready-made sub-samples for a variety of further enquiries. These might include:

- *Admissions of black and mixed parentage children*
The reasons for the disproportionate number of admissions of black children for temporary care warrants further investigation and there is clearly a pressing need to study the reasons for the very high rates of admission and re-admission of young children of mixed parentage. The remarkably small number of Asian children coming into care also requires investigation. It may be that strong family and community support systems make admissions unnecessary. In this case, we all have much to learn from them. It may be, however, that Asian families are not receiving the child care services that they need either because these are not offered in an acceptable way or because they are not aware that such services could be available to them.

- *Multiple admissions*
Multiple admissions to care seem likely to be the experience of a number of young children especially as the concept of shared care takes hold. It seems important to find out how often children are able to return to the same in-care placement and what systems and arrangements best facilitate this.

- *Breakdown rates for older child adoption and long-term fostering placements*
It would be very interesting and helpful if our Year 1 project placements could be followed up in 1990/91 when five years will have elapsed. Some of the Berridge and Cleaver findings could be further explored.

- *Leaving care at 18*
Leaving care for independence is still a relatively unexplored area in spite of some recent studies. It might therefore be instructive to follow up samples of young people who at the time they were discharged were living in flats, lodgings, foster homes or other accommodation, and compare their experiences and adjustment.

- *Reasons for moves in care*
Concern is often expressed about the number of moves in care which children experience. Our large sample should make it possible to examine particular groups of children and investigate the reasons for their moves and the possibility of reducing them.

- *Home on trial*
Findings from the Parker study might be tested against cases in the project sample.

To sum up
The six authorities that participated in this project put a lot of time, energy and commitment into it. We know that individual social workers and their seniors found the experience of completing our questionnaires was often helpful in clarifying plans and we trust that the statistics and reports which we have provided for each participating authority will prove useful to them.

We hope, too, that our work will help people to be more aware of the complexity of evaluating outcome, that as a profession we can become more sophisticated in our concepts of 'success' or 'breakdown' and can learn to avoid making spurious comparisons.

Finally, we hope that the facts, trends and patterns that we have reported here will be of interest and use to managers, practitioners and other researchers and that they will ultimately be of benefit to the children and families who are the recipients of the child care service.

References

1 Goldberg E and Warburton W *Ends and means in social work* Allen & Unwin, 1979.

British Agencies for Adoption & Fostering

British Agencies for Adoption & Fostering (BAAF) is a registered charity and professional association for all those working in the child care field. BAAF's work includes:

providing training and consultation services to social workers and other professionals to help them improve the quality of medical, legal and social work services to children and families;

giving evidence to government committees on subjects concerning children and families;

responding to consultative documents on changes in legislation and regulations affecting children in or at risk of coming into care;

publishing a wide range of books, training packs and leaflets as well as a quarterly journal on adoption, fostering and child care issues;

giving advice and information to members of the public on aspects of adoption, fostering and child care issues;

and helping to find new families for children through the BAAF Exchange Service, 'Be My Parent' and 'Find a Family'.

More information about BAAF (including membership subscription details) can be obtained from BAAF, 11 Southwark Street, London SE1 1RQ.